D0305866

Cotswold Ways

With best wishes from

Cotswold Ways

EDITH BRILL

Edith Brill

Drawings by Michael Stainton

ROBERT HALE · LONDON

Text © Edith Brill 1985
Illustrations © Michael Stainton 1985
First published in Great Britain 1985

Robert Hale Limited
Clerkenwell House
Clerkenwell Green
London EC1R OHT

British Library Cataloguing in Publication Data
Brill Edith
  Cotswold ways.
  1. Cotswold Hills (England) – History
  I. Title
  942.4'17   DA670.C83
  ISBN 0-7090-2379-0

Photoset in Baskerville by
Rowland Phototypesetting Limited, Bury St Edmunds, Suffolk
Printed in Great Britain by
St. Edmundsbury Press, Bury St Edmunds, Suffolk
and bound by Woolnough

Contents

To Wendy, Mary M., Mary J. and N. S.
(*Good travellers all!*)

Illustrations

1 · Introduction

The boundaries of Cotswold differ according to who defines them. An estate agent, for example, aware that 'Cotswold' has become an emotive word in the last few decades, has a more flexible range, but a Cotsaller or true lover of the region knows when he is in his own country, for his eyes tell him in a myriad different revelations. It has to do with the way the hills fold into each other, the colour of the ploughed earth, wet or dry, the drystone walling following the contours, the quality of light emanating from land and sky, and such small details as a finial on a gable, a carved bracket holding a door-hood, the rough stone of a gatepost showing the white and yellow circles of lichen growth.

For those who prefer more definite boundaries, Cotswold comes within that belt of oolitic limestone lying diagonally between the Humber and the Dorset coast, the highest and widest part being in Gloucestershire. For me the heart of the region, some forty miles wide and twenty broad, ranges from north of Wotton-under-Edge, east of Gloucester and Cheltenham, with Burford and Lechlade in the south. The farther one gets from the centre, the more diluted the Cotswold influence, though a Tudor manor-house or a cottage that could have been lifted out of the Swells can bring to the exile nostalgia for that land of lost content, the hills of home.

This boundary covers more ground than the original definition, for in the beginning it was the name given to the high wolds between Winchcombe and Stow-on-the-Wold and was derived not only from the Anglo-Saxon for 'high, open land' but from Cod, who was a Saxon chief who settled there some fourteen hundred years ago. The valley became 'Cod's dene' or 'Cutsdean', and the hill country above became 'Cotswold'. As the centuries passed, the name came to be used for the south of the region also, and it must have been firmly established by 1791, for Bigland wrote at that time of 'Bisley, near

Stroud, the last parish of that division of the Country called Cotswold'.

One would like to know if Cod used the stone beneath his feet, but no traces of buildings have been recognized as belonging to him. One would like to think he visited Belas Knap, the long barrow above Winchcombe, for it would have told him how neolithic man, some three thousand years before the Saxon invasions, had used drystone walling for the barrow's curving false entrance, placing one sliver of stone less than an inch thick upon another so that a knife blade could not be inserted between them, making mortar to hold them together unnecessary.

Nearly half of the region lies within the 400–600 feet contours, with the remainder rising to 950 feet, while a few points on the northern and western scarp exceed 1,000 feet. Looked at from beyond Severn, the escarpment appears to form an unbroken bastion of hills on the horizon. South from Birdlip its slopes begin to be covered with beechwoods, beautiful at all times of the year, in the tender greenery of May, the heavy fleece of summer, the russets of autumn when colour smoulders not only on the boughs but beneath them, and perhaps best of all in winter, when pale sunlight slants down to give a pewter lustre to the smooth, upstanding trunks.

At Stroud, Dursley and Wotton-under-Edge the uplands are furrowed into long, winding valleys or bottoms that, looked at from a distance, have a dramatic, almost theatrical aspect despite a certain amount of industrial sprawl. From the escarpment on a clear day the Severn estuary and its river can be seen in the middle distance, while beyond are the mountains of Wales, making it easy to imagine how Caractacus and his men, fleeing from the Romans, could cross the Severn at Arlingham or thereabouts and reach the haven of the Welsh mountains. They would know how to avoid the Severn's treacherous reaches where at low tide the complex currents and whirlpools under the banks at Arlingham can trap the unknowing. (In Saxon times this place was called Unla, a Saxon word meaning misfortune.) Later, when the West Saxons had beaten the Celts at the Battle of Dyrham in AD577 and the land between Severn and Cotswold was open to the victors, the Celts fled across the river at a point where it almost curls back on itself, and there the pursuing West Saxons tried to cut them off by swimming across to the other side, but, not realizing the treachery of the waters at this point, most of them were drowned.

There are many stories told about the Severn crossings, the most recent being of a man who forded it near Arlingham to prove it was still possible, but the story I like best comes from Bigland's *Collections*, 1786. It tells how King Edward the Elder, lying at Aust Clive, invited Leolin, Prince of Wales, to a conference to settle a dispute, but Leolin, suspicious of the King, refused to cross the river, whereupon Edward crossed the Severn himself, though as the more powerful of the two he could have insisted Leolin came to him. Ashamed of his suspicions, Leolin was moved to make amends, and before King Edward's boat reached the shore he leapt into the water and embraced the King, saying: 'Most wise King, your humility has conquered my pride, your wisdom triumphed over my folly. Mount that neck which I have foolishly exalted against you and enter that country which your goodness this day has made your own.' Taking Edward on his shoulders, he carried him ashore. It would be difficult to imagine affairs of state conducted in this fashion today!

In north Cotswold the contours of the hills are more subtle, flowing in long, gentle ridges sometimes crowned with rounded clumps of beech, though these grow less each year through over-ripeness and decay, most having been planted by landowners to commemorate Trafalgar or Waterloo or the coming of age of an heir. From Cleeve Cloud above Cheltenham, there is the recognizable bulk of the Malverns beyond lesser hills, and where the steep lane from Winchcombe comes out at Roel Gate one looks across at the Bredons, the Malverns and the blue mists of distant Wales, while from Dover's Hill, that last outlier of Cotswold, Meon Hill and its Iron Age encampment rise broad-based out of the plain north-east of Chipping Campden.

Perhaps because of its isolated position, Meon Hill has gathered about itself vague sinister stories of witchcraft and ritual killing. These could have originated in folklore or from the Victorian love of the gruesome, helped by a modern tragedy distorted by rumour to an indefinable horror. In the summer holidays I could see Meon Hill from my bedroom window, but when I wanted to go there I was told I must never venture there alone, that it was hostile to strangers and had no road for the pony cart. I discovered years later that there were tracks on the hill which might have been used to transport the iron currency bars belonging to the Iron Age that had been found there. There may also have been a track between Meon Hill and Salmonsbury Camp near Bourton-on-the-Water, for the same kind of currency bars have been found at Salmonsbury.

Meon Hill has never lost its faint aura of mystery for me, so that

Escarpment view from Broadway Tower westwards

when I see it from the road to Stratford-upon-Avon I can still feel a faint thrill of apprehension. As late as the 1960s I was told that every Midsummer Eve detectives came to 'lurk' in local pubs hoping to discover evidence of witchcraft or evil practices. How exactly they 'lurked' I was unable to discover. I imagined detectives with hat brims turned down and coat collars turned up skulking behind beer barrels, but knowing countrymen I am sure no stranger would remain undetected for long or find out very much, for the locals invariably clam up when questioned by inquisitive outsiders.

Until the nineteenth century Cotswold was a complete industrial as well as a complete geological unit, its natural resources combining to earn its livelihood. The abundant supply of stone was easily quarried, each parish having its own quarry and some supplying fissile stone suitable for roofing slates. Below were the oolite layers of fuller's earth for fulling the cloth, while the porous nature of the rock also meant that surface water no longer able to seep through burst out as springs where the limestone met the fuller's earth. This meant that springs of pure, clean water were available for domestic and industrial use, while the streams and little rivers provided power and, in the case of the Windrush at least, transported stone between the quarries at Barrington, Taynton and Burford to the limits of the region where the Windrush joined the Thames and so on to London.

Because of the porous nature of the subsoil, the sward of the sheep-walks was sweet and clean, a mixture of herbs and grasses kept delicate by the nibbling of the sheep, and this good pasture improved the quality of the wool which made England famous in the Middle Ages. The wealth it brought to the wool-men helped to pay for the building of such churches as those at Chipping Campden, Northleach, Fairford and many another, for the wool-men hoped their benefactions would ease their entry into Heaven after death. Also, because of their close contact with the Low Countries, Cotswold was enriched by European ideas of architecture, art and culture, the wool-men being as much at home in Flanders and Calais as they were in England. Even the peasants gained something from this trade in wool. Many of them managed to keep a few sheep on common land and to sell the wool to the factors who came at shearing time to buy quantities large or small. Sometimes, when the demand was great, they were glad of scraping together as many fleeces as possible by any means.

When the wool trade gave way to the trade in cloth, England benefited greatly by the arrival of Flemish weavers persecuted for their faith in their own country who fled to England. As the manufacture got under way, cloth instead of wool was exported, the rivers and streams providing the power, and here again local conditions provided the necessary elements to make the Stroudwater Reds, the Uley Blues, and the fine black broadcloth that was so hardwearing that suits made from it were handed down from father to son.

The clothing trade prospered greatly, producing several generations of gentlemen clothiers, some of whom used their wealth to buy manors and manor-houses in decay from ancient landowning families, getting out of the cloth business while the going was still good, for it was a trade that did not last.

By the end of the eighteenth century the rot had set in, and at the beginning of the nineteenth century trade had been steadily eroded and finally killed by the mills of the north using steam power and factory methods to produce the greater amounts of cheaper, more fancy kinds of cloth demanded by the increasing population. The clothiers of south Cotswold, unwilling or unable to change over to steam power and cheaper cloth or from lack of capital, after many bankruptcies had to recognize that the days of cloth-making on Cotswold were over, though in the Stroud area a few enterprising mill-owners went over to steam power. Thousands of spinners, weavers, tuckers, combers and others were thrown out of work, and there was much hardship on Cotswold. Families starved, some managed to emigrate, others fled to work in the mills of the north of England. The decline occurred at the time of the Enclosures, so that the weavers lost not only their jobs but the right to keep a cow or a few geese on common land, which had at one time supplemented their earnings. They could not work on the land: their hands were too delicate, having been kept smooth for their work; their physical condition was generally poor, because of the sedentary lives they had led, and the agricultural workers themselves were so poorly paid that many had to have parish relief to enable them to feed their families, though they worked long hours. Cotswold's one-time importance in the national economy was forgotten, and it became a remote region, difficult of access because of its 'wild rough hills and rough uneven ways' as anyone who remembers the narrow lanes winding up the steep hillsides before the last world war can testify.

2 · *Cotswold Vernacular*

It is less than a hundred years since William Morris discovered that in the little towns and villages of Cotswold unbroken traditions of building and other crafts still survived, methods of work and skills passed on from those masons who built the great religious houses, the Perpendicular churches, the manor-houses and the tithe barns.

Before the twentieth century, visitors came not because they enjoyed the scene but because they had business on Cotswold needing their presence: abbots travelling between their abbeys and their manors at sheep-shearing and harvest to see all was safely gathered in their great barns, pilgrims worshipping at the shrines at Winchcombe and Hailes, merchants of the Staple buying wool, drovers from Wales bringing cattle along the green roads for the London market, pedlars and other itinerants travelling the Jurassic Way across Britain. Indeed, from journals and letters it would seem that most of them endured Cotswold country because they must.

Daniel Defoe came on one of his Tours, but his mind was on the clothing trade and other industries. Alexander Pope in the eighteenth century expressed appreciation of the pleasures of Cirencester Park but he was occupied with Lord Bathurst changing the landscape. William Cobbett in his *Rural Rides*, published in 1830, wrote: 'This wold is in itself an ugly country having less to please the eye than any other I have seen.' Yet if he had not been such a kind-hearted, self-opinionated old buffer, angered by the poor conditions of the Cotswold farm labourer, he might have realized that his overall description of 'the long stretches of upland, the winding valleys, the clear trout streams and the grey venerable hamlets dotted along their banks . . . are all marks of a strange land marked off by its particular genius from the outside everyday world' was an appreciation not a criticism, though I doubt if his natural perversity would have let him acknowledge it. The beauty he appreciated was to be found in good

Elizabethan Manor at Upper Slaughter, once the parsonage, home of the Witt family.

cottages, rosy-cheeked children and men and women not worn down by the struggle to keep body and soul together.

Inspired by William Morris and caught up in the same medieval entanglement, master craftsmen such as Ernest Gimson, the Barnsley brothers and Norman Jewson came to live and work on Cotswold. Being an articulate company, they began to make known their discovery of a medieval enclave in the hills, and the image that so many people associate with Cotswold was born. It was also the beginning of the tourist trade, attracting artists, writers, poets and others who deplored the soulless way industry was progressing and who were disgusted by the badly designed goods turned out. They in their turn helped to perpetuate the Cotswold image.

It was an image based on the Elizabethan or medieval features of the manor-houses, farm buildings and cottages, consisting of gables, mullioned and transomed window openings, dormers, steep-pitched

9

Cotswold

roofs with their darker-toned slates beginning with the largest at the eaves and becoming gradually smaller as they ascended to the roof-ridge, the drip-moulds and labels, the finials, the carved brackets and the massive chimneys, with the humblest cottage showing an affinity with the manor-house because the same oolitic limestone quarried nearby had provided the material for all the local building.

The siting of the villages in the valleys seems perfect – each valley with its own sparkling stream or river, the dwellings grouped around a Perpendicular-towered church with its churchyard trees, or, where the valley was very narrow, perched on a hillside and snuggling down into any natural shelf or shallow hollow for shelter in what appears haphazard fashion; one cannot imagine them in any other position. They had a beauty that C. F. Innocent, in his *Development of English Building Construction*, describes as 'a spontaneous product of the hands of their constructors who were in a state of culture in which technical ability produced works of art naturally and unselfconsciously, unlike the technically skilled workers of the present day who can only design "works of art" after training'.

The core is still there, as beguiling as ever – even two world wars have not extinguished it, and that is what most visitors come to see, though the villages are no longer completely 'grey and venerable', nor would one wish them to be. One cannot bring back a style that has lost its true reason for existing, nor keep the original vitality of a tradition outworn.

Until the middle of the nineteenth century there were positive reasons for the Cotswold vernacular. The roofs that give such a picturesque finish to an old house were steep pitched so that the rain would run off them quickly, the stone slates being porous and Cotswold prone to violent, heavy rains in summer and snow in winter that must not be allowed to lie on the roof or it would seep through and under the slates. It was necessary to use the stone because it was at hand and to be had for the cost of quarrying, and because of the difficulties of transporting any other material such as bricks and timber on the poorly surfaced, steep and often narrow roads of the uplands. The slates could be taken from shallow pits dug just below the ground, though for freestone of good quality deeper quarrying was necessary. As Cotswold is practically one huge quarry, the pits were often dug near field gateways, making it easier to convey the stone to the road. And then there were the mason's own individual touches, the need of man to assure himself he does not live by bread alone but must project his own personality on his work by the

Kingston minerals: quarry at Stumps Cross above Stanway

addition of a porch or hood-mould to distinguish it from its fellows. The weathering of the stone adds its own patina, and good craftsmanship shows in every part, walls, chimneys, ornamentation and that most important part of a roof, the swept alley where two angles join, always a vulnerable place where the rain can get through.

The decoration is never overstressed. One comes to recognize that the style is not wholly Tudor, Renaissance, Georgian or Victorian but a vernacular that can contain them all harmoniously because the building material comes from the local quarry. It takes a long time for a legend to die, many of us clinging obstinately to our idea of Cotswold and perpetuating a pallid imitation of the style and the stone we have learnt to love, for it is the cosiest, most homely looking of all the domestic architecture Britain has ever produced.

The transition from the Tudor style to the Classical Renaissance of the early eighteenth century for the more important houses began

Medford House, Mickleton in Queen Anne style

in many instances by putting a classical façade on an old building, but one of the best examples I know of a building erected as a whole embodying the old and new is Medford House in Mickleton, a large village under the northern edge unhappily situated on the main ·Stratford to Birmingham road. Originally Mickleton had a kinship with the Vale, as seen in the few picturesque timber-framed houses remaining, and an affinity with the hills in its good stone houses. Today most of the village has been taken over by new housing estates of indeterminate design so the older houses seem almost an intrusion. Medford House, built in 1694, is a blend of the styles of Queen Elizabeth and Queen Anne. The blend is pleasing, the hipped roof with dormers has taken the place of gables, and the entrance has Renaissance ornament. When I last saw it, I wished I had a magician's power to transport it to a gracious town street where it could exist side by side with its own kind instead of looking out of place and forgotten, surviving in as dignified a manner as possible.

Kiftsgate Stone above Chipping Campden

3 · The Valley of the Coln

The River Coln belongs to Cotswold entirely, beginning and ending within its boundaries. It rises on Wantley Farm below Charlton Abbots in the parish of Sevenhampton and flows south-west to Lechlade, where it is taken into the Thames.

The monks of Winchcombe Abbey had a hospice for lepers at Charlton Abbots, travelling there by the Salt Way linking Winchcombe with Sherborne and turning west at the crossroads at Roel Gate to follow a lesser Salt Way that served Charlton Abbots. Where the hospice once stood, a spring bubbled into a large stone trough, one of the many springs feeding the infant river. I remember years ago drinking from it after a long, hot walk over the wolds, and this water has stayed in my mind as the coldest and sweetest I have ever known. Certainly the lepers would have had invigorating air and fresh water to sustain them.

The Coln is not much more than a trickle as it comes to the secluded valley where Sevenhampton stands. In 1490 its church was enriched and enlarged by John Combar, wool-merchant of Worcester. When he died he asked to be buried in Sevenhampton, a district to which he had often travelled buying fleeces and fells. He left money in his will to build a Perpendicular tower, north and south transepts and a porch. It is the way the tower has been inserted, with separate piers and flying buttresses across the transepts, that gives the church its special grace.

The infant Coln becomes a fair-sized brook in the two miles it takes to come to Syreford, the ancient ford of the pigs. Here it is channelled into a deep ditch by the roadside, flowing with the road to a right-hand track leading to an ancient mill. The ford has disappeared but there are signs of its former location in disturbed muddy ground as the stream leaves the road to disappear from sight in a rough copse. There is an old house much renovated on the

Mill pool on the Coln

opposite side of the turning into the track with an outside flight of worn stone steps looking strangely purposeless now the building they once served has been changed out of recognition. It looks as if the building could have been a farmhouse or a mill.

The sides of the track leading off the road have been planted with shrubs to look like a drive, and the little brook has disappeared behind the shrubbery. At the end of the track, as it comes to a disused mill, the brook is lost in the woodland and joins up with other watercourses that once provided the power to turn the water-wheel. This attempt at making an ornamental drive out of an old track that once led to the mill in a situation as well watered as this can be successful only if it is watched closely. Nature is waiting to overrun it again, and when it does, the water-plants that line a Cotswold brook, the reeds and rushes, willowherb and loosestrife, will return.

The Coln goes through Andoversford keeping company with the railway, the river covering more mileage than the railway track as it meanders lazily in the open where marsh and water-birds strut and feed in the shallows of small curving bays. At Withington it is lost to view in the woods and is not free again to reflect the sky until it has left the woods and plantations of Stowele Park behind and come to Coln St Denis. The river worked a large mill at Withington which is now an inn.

There is so much history and prehistory to be learned about Withington that one could write as many pages as there are trees in its splendid hanging woods. It existed in Saxon times, for a resident priest is mentioned in Domesday Book; it had an abbey that was sacked in 877 by the Danes and never rebuilt, but before that there is evidence that even at that early period the wool gathered from the sheep-walks in the vicinity was exported. Coming to the fifteenth century, the Perpendicular tower of its church has a special elegance, suggesting that the wealth had come from wool, though we do not know the name of the benefactor. A fascinating memorial difficult to see because it is high on the south-west end is of Sir John Howe of Cassey Compton (who died in 1657) and his family; they appear as if seated in a box at the opera, and on closer scrutiny one sees they are holding skulls and other symbols of death, a contrast the sculptor must have intended.

Cobbett was not very pleased with Withington. When he visited it in 1820, although he found it 'prettily situated', he remarked that, '. . . it was, and not so very long ago, a gay and happy place; but it now presents a picture of dilapidation and shabbiness scarcely to be equalled.' Looking at the tastefully modernized cottages, the glossy cars outside the inn, it is difficult to imagine this today, or the tales told about farm labourers who in the nineteenth century turned

Cotswold cattle and Old Spots at Cassey Compton

poachers to feed their families, their meagre wages being insufficient
to do this. A poacher suffered cruel penalties if caught for he was
considered a bigger villain by the local landowners than any cut-
throat criminal. James Joy, from Withington (did he ever wonder at
the irony of his name?), was sentenced to seven years transportation
in 1833 even though there was no fighting at his capture and nobody
was injured.

The villages of Chedworth and Withington lie close to Romano-
British sites. Their names suggest Anglo-Saxon origins, and they
probably existed before the Romans came, for it seems natural that
when settlers found an estate in being, even if it had fallen out of
cultivation, it would be easier to take it over than break new ground.
They would also take over any peasants who remained, and one
master must have been pretty much like another to peasants tied to
the land. The work would be the same, ploughing and sowing,
reaping and winnowing, animals to be fed, water carried, wood .

chopped. Professor Finburg, in his *Gloucestershire*, notes that these parishes may preserve in their boundaries the outline of Romano-British estates.

Chedworth even had a railway which ran between Cheltenham and Swindon. In a clearing just beyond the Chedworth Roman Villa (one of several on the Coln's banks), the railway embankment has become part of the woodland scene, with ferns and cushions of moss, brambles and clumps of willow-herb under the hazel wands. There is evidence in the Roman villa that the occupants fulled cloth and washed wool using the clean waters of the Coln, and that there was a temple to a water-goddess or nymph so that the giver of this precious source of life could be worshipped. When the Saxons took over, none knew better than they the value of a good water-supply, probably using the river as a source of transport when they had established themselves at Bibury, for the church of Coln Rogers is evidence of their settlement in the neighbourhood.

The Coln disappears under the Foss Way at Foss Bridge before coming into Coln St Denis and Coln Rogers, villages whose stones are mossy with damp river airs, the houses secluded within the shrubberies and tall trees of their gardens, while along the line of the river willow and poplar trees turn their silvery undersides in the breeze.

From Coln Rogers one can walk along a grassy track and under woods to cross the river by a wooden bridge, the kind of bridge where one is tempted to linger in blissful indolence hypnotized by the sparkle of the water or waiting for the kingfisher who haunts these reaches, and so come to the lower end of Calcot, a hamlet on the open hillside. The roofs, dormers and gables of the cottages make a fascinating collection of triangular shapes ascending the hill, and each cottage has some slight difference from its neighbour to set it apart; one has the rounded shape of an old bread oven on its walls. In recent years the cottages have been smartened and modernized, but not aggressively so, and it is still the little grey hamlet of farmworkers' cottages on a pale, open hillside, though I doubt if the cottages are now inhabited by farmworkers as they were sixty years ago.

The contrast between the deep colours of Coln Rogers hidden amongst its screen of trees and the pale tints of Calcot is one of the happy surprises of Cotswold landscape. I came to Calcot one summer day after a night of fierce showers – Cotswold weather we used to call it, the kind that turns hillside paths into tumbling rivers and

Calcot

then the water disappears quickly and there is barely a trace of it to be seen except tiny drops on grass blades jewelled by the sun. The blue of the sky was so intense I dared not look up at it, and clouds with silvered edges sent shadows of themselves chasing over the hillside, advancing and retreating like dancers in a folk ritual: a perfect day for Cotswold, which needs the sun to light up its stone and give it back its golden or silver colour. The rain-washed air made every detail clear: the lichen on a stone, tall spikes of mullein with buds tightly buttoned to the stem, harebells, scabious, purple knapweed in the grassy wayside. There was a clump of viper's bugloss, not a common flower on Cotswold, with red, blue and pink buds and flowers hanging out of their silver-bristled sheaths. As we walked up the village street, we saw a handsome, aristocratic spaniel with long black ears, not unlike the china dogs one sees in antique shops today but which a hundred years ago, when these cottages were inhabited by farmworkers, probably graced the mantelshelf, having been won at Stow Fair. He was looking with doggy hauteur out of a cottage window and did not condescend to bark but watched as we went past, looking down from the window, which was some three feet from the ground. Evidently he did not think it dignified to jump down like any ordinary dog but had his own little pair of wooden steps, or perhaps he was too old. Not wishing to hurt his feelings, we refrained from laughing until we were well out of hearing, but this comicality pleased us, as did everything about this part of Coln River.

Coln Rogers is a tiny village secluded in a landscape of lush waterside meadows, silver willows, ancient trees. The church escaped the Victorian restorers, and its Saxon origin is written plain in the four pilaster strips which have stepped bases, long and short quoins at all angles of the nave and a tiny round-headed north window. In the churchyard is a modern headstone by Simon Verity to David Talbot Rice, 1903–72, 'Byzantine Scholar and much-loved countryman'; above his name is a splendid bull in relief, at the sides a shovel and hammer, at the foot a hayrake; there is no need for more. Also in the churchyard is a memorial that says twenty-five men and one woman from the village went to the war and all came back. Looking at it, the lift of the heart came again and we silently echoed the words on the Memorial: Thanks be to God!

Ablington, the village of high walls that any waller would have been proud to have built, has clipped yews, houses with lawns and gardens where the Coln has been tamed to enhance gracious living, vistas of hanging willow wands over quiet, shining water. It has turned Cotswold vernacular into Cotswold Particular or even Cotswold Glamorous, for the residents are determined to preserve their privacy from the thousands of summer visitors to Bibury, a mile or so down the road. But even so, they might have made it possible for the water to continue to flow so a thirsty wayfarer could drink at the 1914–18 war memorial, a tap in a rectangular recess in the wall at the edge of the road. The memorial was made not only as a place where thirst might be quenched and as a reminder of the beautiful river that has given the village its beauty but because at that time many of the cottages had no inside water-supply of fresh water, so this tap would be a boon to them. But now the tap is turned off, and water no longer flows from it. It is reached by a semi-circular flight of shallow steps plain but pleasant to the eye and made, I hope, by some village mason. Those who remember the dead of the First

World War grow fewer every day; the men who went to war have passed into history. All that is left of Ablington's village memorial is four names and a simple inscription on a small bronze tablet, and four graduated steps made by a mason who shaped Cotswold stone as masons have done down the centuries.

Ablington Manor, one of the most outstanding small manor-houses on Cotswold, was built in 1599 by John Coxwell. It was later the home of Arthur Gibbs, whose books, *A Cotswold Village*, first published in 1898, is now a classic. He was no bucolic squire but a scholar who imbued his country sports with a classical aura.

An earlier writer, Charles Coxwell, rector of Bibury in the early nineteenth century, has nothing to do with Cotswold as we know it today, but his book of reminiscences and family history, privately printed, can bring a pang of nostalgia to those who prefer old ways and old days, in theory at least. His family home was Ablington Manor, and he kept the Bibury rectorship warm for the younger son of the lord of the manor, Sackville Cresswell, until he could take Holy Orders. Coxwell seems to have been a bumbling, garrulous, kindly man, who, when he wrote of himself in his book, used the third person, looking down on himself with the same kindliness as he looked down on his parishioners: '. . . he declined the exercise of hunting though situated in the neighbourhood of hounds, but was fond of shooting albeit he was a very indifferent marksman as being near-sighted . . . he had some knowledge of music and performed but poorly on the violin and for singing he had no talent at all . . . in his department as magistrate he was accessible to all . . . in every case which would admit it he inclined to Mercy and never signed a Warrant of Commitment to Prison but with reluctance.'

Coming out of the tree-shaded road from Ablington into Bibury, one also comes out into a new world of light reflected from the shining expanse of the wide river with its background of woods, ancient grey cottages and old stone bridge with the bastioned mill at one end and its church perched high above the river at the other end. If one can see Bibury without too much traffic getting in the way, one understands why William Morris called it the most beautiful village on Cotswold. The famous Arlington Row, the picturebook group, has been beautifully restored so that it looks more Cotswold than ever, but it has had its surrounding marshes drained away, and the occupants no longer look out of their windows to water immediately below. (When young I remember being told by an old man, to amuse a child, of how he used to lean out of his window and

24

spear a trout for breakfast.) The Racks, used for drying cloth when the Row was a medieval wool-hall, have lost their marshy ground, once the home of ragged robins, reeds and other water-loving plants.

The fishermen have the best of it, being the most unobtrusive of people, hiding away in the loneliest reaches of the river from morning to early evening, when they return to discuss their catches, or non-catches, with their own kind, being no trouble to anyone at all except on occasions the fish.

When it leaves Bibury, the Coln flows south-east through woods and parkland to make an abrupt turn to pass Coln St Aldwyn and then goes due south to Quenington, its last village before it reaches Fairford and the Thames. Quenington is a good-sized village not submerged in the past or too self-consciously kept there. It has a higher and a lower part, with new housing estates in the upper part for an expanding population as well as a country industry, Godwin's water-pump factory, established over a hundred years. This industry finds work for the young men of the village and helps keep it alive.

The more ancient part of Quenington is reached by a road out of the large village green descending into the valley. On the way down one passes a high gatehouse, plain except for a canopied niche holding a small weatherworn figure, and this gateway is all that remains of a preceptory belonging to the Knights Templars who owned much of the land around Quenington in 1338 and who took many a thousand fleeces from sheep grazing on the hills above.

The old church of St Swithin's is at the bottom of the hill, near where the river runs and where one can stand by the bridge and see the water shadowed by drooping willow wands and the exotic trees of a private garden. The church stands in a bright emerald lawn. The few carved headstones that have been preserved have been ranged in a row under the low wall surrounding the lawn so one gets a feeling that the churchyard plays an unimportant role in the village except as a meeting place.

It is improbable that the two elaborately carved Romanesque doorways of about 1150 could have been given by the Knights Templars, because the doorways were there some fifty years before the estate was given to them by Agnes de Lacy in 1193. According to learned opinion, the south doorway is by the sculptor responsible for the doorway at South Cerney, and the late Professor David Talbot Rice wrote that the sculptures in all probability belonged to the reign

Footbridge from Arlington Row, Bibury

of Stephen (1135–54). They look so remote from the world today that fifty years or so can make little difference to their dating now. The tympanum shows the rare Coronation of the Virgin enclosed in a chevron moulding which also continues down the jambs. The next order is that of beakheads, and round the arch they are mostly of animals but on the jamb shafts they go into the stylized forms with clasping tongues. The north doorway is even more elaborate, having four orders, an inner arch with chevrons, a band of limpet shells, star, cable, knot and billet mouldings, while the jambs have large daisy-like flowers. The tympanum shows the Harrowing of Hell. One of the three naked figures is half in a devil's mouth, while above is a sun disk with a face to it.

Apart from the two doorways, the church is so altered that little is left to give a sense of continuity with the years when the doorways were carved, though judging by some pieces of carved stone isolated on a wall it must have had much more decoration. The interior is uncluttered, undistinguished and without the usual odour that clings to an ancient church like the lichen on its walls, but it has the most charming collection of embroidered kneelers of any Cotswold church, representing the wild flowers and birds of the neighbourhood. Today the two Romanesque doorways, despite their positions, do not seem to belong to the rest of the building. They are of such a different cast of ideas that they have become alien, just as the two worlds of Quenington, its hopeful-looking new housing estates around the green and the remains of its past by the riverside, do not seem to have anything to say to each other.

Leaving Quenington, the Coln comes to Fairford, and now the Cotswold influence has become fainter, though Fairford's wool-church belongs to the hills. It was entirely rebuilt between 1485 and 1500 by John Tame, a wool-merchant who died before it was completed; his son Edmund finished it as an act of filial piety. John Tame had become wealthy through the wool-trade, but as he became richer and more important he remembered his origins and decorated his handsome church tower not only with the arms of the noble families of the district but with the symbols of trade connected with the town, including the cockleshell emblem of the salt-trader who came along the Salt Way from Droitwich to ship his product at Fairford on the Thames *en route* for London. The twenty-six windows of the church are filled with painted glass flooding the

Norman doorway, Quenington

Valentine Strong's tomb, Fairford

interior with reflections of rich colour. They tell Bible stories from
the Garden of Eden to the Acts of the Apostles. The glass has been
taken out and hidden several times down the centuries to save it
from the hazards of wars, including the last. There is evidence that
the complete set came from the same glass-house and was designed
and painted by Barnard Flower, the glass-painter of Henry VII.

Fairford's other connection with Cotswold history is of an earlier
date. Some hundred years ago a Saxon cemetery of at least 130
graves was discovered west of the town, the skeletons being of men
over six feet and some over six feet six inches. One local newspaper
at the time called it a 'Graveyard of the Giants'. The cemetery is a
strong link in the chain of evidence of the direction the advance
across Cotswold the Saxon settlers took in the sixth century.

Today Fairford is best known for its fishing and ever-increasing
flooded gravel-pits now used for recreation, giving sanctuary to wild
birds as well as pleasure to those who enjoy water-sports.

28

In Fairford Park the Coln is artificially widened and then, free once more, it comes out into the rushy meadows of Inglesham, soon to mingle its waters with the Thames.

4 · The Evenlode Valley

From its source in Batsford Park near Moreton-in-Marsh, the river Evenlode for the most part of its south-easterly journey makes a dividing line between Gloucestershire and Oxfordshire Cotswold.

> A lovely river, all alone
>> She lingers in the hills and holds
> A hundred little towns of stone
>> Forgotten in the western wolds

sang Hilaire Belloc. Today these little towns of stone are far less lonely and forgotten, but they still keep some of the magic they had for Belloc: one can still find an old stone bridge to lean over, a church with a Norman doorway and a churchyard where headstones hoary with lichen lean amongst the grass and yew trees, willows wave their long tassels over the water and coots and moorhens paddling in and out of the shadows at the water's edge.

The river comes to Moreton-in-Marsh in less than two miles. 'Henmarsh' was the old name for the little town, and marshy it certainly was at one time, being regularly flooded at the east end of the town until the road was raised. Ogilvy's road map shows the district to be a morass in 1675. Some experts say the name came from 'marc' meaning 'boundary'; perhaps both meanings might apply.

For centuries Moreton has been a port of call for travellers as an important through-way, and being on the Foss it was granted a charter in 1330 by the abbot of Worcester to hold a market on Saturdays. The people of Moreton let this privilege lapse for many years, but the market has been revived in recent years, and it is interesting that opposition to the re-opening lost the case when it was debated and the ancient right was upheld. Now for one day in the week the wide street is alive with the press of people about the stalls, with noise, litter, traffic jams, cheapjackery, people hugging unwieldly bags and bundles and bumping into each other, the smell of chips and hamburgers replacing that of the delicacies of medieval England – though probably those were just as odorous.

As befits a town on a through route, Moreton has its inns, the earliest the Manor Hotel dating from 1656, while the White Hart is said to be one of the inns where Charles I slept, in 1644. The Resedale Arms, named after the family who once owned Batsford, was one of the principal inns of the eighteenth century and not only served travellers but its public rooms were used for balls and assemblies of all kinds for the local gentry.

Moreton is also the railway centre of the region, and Lord Resedale did the people of today good service when he stipulated that every passenger train should stop at its station. Ominous rumblings from time to time start rumours about closing down the route, but so far petitions have prevailed and commuters to London and Oxford keep their lifeline. Another little railway running from Moreton to Stratford-upon-Avon has vanished. It was opened in 1860 for goods traffic between the two places. A local parson, Francis Witt, in an entry in his diary for 8 September 1860 comments: '. . . vast concourse of people assembled at Moreton-in-Marsh . . . at an early hour in the evening all the provisions of the town were exhausted, the roasted ox demolished and neither bread or beer to be had for love or money. The committee preceded the coal waggons with a band of music and all was joyous. Behind the scenes, however, the proprietors have reason to mourn over mismanagement, exhausted means and scant hopes even of distant renumeration; but the public will no doubt be considerable gainers.' Does the entry imply that Reverend Francis Witt had a poor opinion of the enterprise?

Railway history tells the story of the Battle of Mickleton tunnel, when the railway was in the making. Tunnelling through the rock at Mickleton began in 1844, and it was six years before it was completed. Trouble with the contractors was responsible for some of the delay for there were fierce disputes between them and Brunel, who, after the contractor's men occupied the workings and refused to come out, brought in some two thousand of his navvies from the Black Country and Ireland to expel them by force. Local people used to talk of this battle as one of the wonders of the century, but two world wars have overlaid its memory.

The Evenlode, when it has left Moreton, flows south-easterly, fed by small tributaries from the water-meadows between Evenlode

Tuesday Market, Moreton-in-Marsh

village and Adlestrop. Evenlode church has a fourteenth-century wooden pulpit of wineglass shape in its medieval church and some good stone houses, but the river has the greater charm. It flows on past Adlestrop where the name-board of a lost railway station is preserved – I like to think because of Edward Thomas's famous poem, but it may be, of course, a gesture by a railway enthusiast. In the old rectory Jane Austen used to stay with her uncle Theophilus Leigh, rector of Adlestrop for forty years, but one cannot recognize it from any description in her novels as one of those country houses where her characters lived or visited, for they are composite places with their shrubberies for gentle walks and parlours where elegant young ladies wrote letters or worked at their embroidery.

Oddington, on the opposite side of the river, has two churches. The elder, St Nicholas, nearly half a mile from the village down a rough track, has trees about it, giving the impression of its being in hiding, and at dusk one can imagine the trees closing in on it. In the late nineteenth century it must have been even more remote from the life of the village, for it stood unused and forlorn with the creatures of the wild finding shelter there. St Francis, I feel, would not have been as shocked as the people who discovered a vixen with a nest of cubs in the fine Jacobean pulpit. Today it has been cleaned up and a large Doom painting on the north wall restored to some of its former brightness. It is more individual in its conception than the usual Doom paintings. There is a devil blowing up Hell's fire with his bellows, an angel helping a poor soul trying to reach Heaven, and, strangely, some of the doomed wear crowns. Score-marks on the stone benches of the porch are said to have been made by archers sharpening their arrows; sceptics might question this, but tradition has been known to embody truth, and the story does conjure up a picture of archers clad as in the Bayeux Tapestry setting off from Oddington to fight the Normans.

When it has passed Daylesford, the Evenlode receives many little brooks, and past Kingham, Churchill and Bledington the Westcote Brook makes a large contribution as the river comes into Wychwood forest country, that 'furtive ungodly place' Joanna Cannon called it, and others have said the same.

Kingham was the village loved by Warde Fowler, the Oxford ornothologist, and at one time it was said he knew every wild bird that lived on the long spur of Daylesford Hill and the woods, meadows and streams under it. Kingham also has a family of blacksmiths famous for wrought-iron gates.

Doom wall-painting, Oddington, St Nicholas

Though Bledington, some 2½ miles south of Oddington, is in Gloucestershire, the Cotswold influence is fading. It once belonged to Winchcombe Abbey, and it could be that the abbey's masons were responsible for the outstanding excellence of some of the work of its church's interior. Apart from the church the village is disappointing as a Cotswold village, but there are some pleasant stone-built houses on one side of the green, and the green itself gives the village the necessary focal point.

Stonesfield's affinity with Cotswold today is mostly underground, for this is where the famous stone slates came from. The village stands in that kind of bleak Oxfordshire landscape which I feel has never recovered from late nineteenth-century privations. W. S. Arkell's book *Oxford Stone* explains the history of the quarries in fascinating detail. It was a chancy business, though in most years work at the quarries provided bread if not jam for local workers. Return for their work, however, depended on hard winter frosts for the quarried stone could be rendered useless in a mild winter – that is, if the water between the layers of stone did not freeze and so ultimately let the stone split into thin layers ready to be shaped into slates or roofing tiles. There are few signs of this industry to be seen in the village today, for most of the mineshafts have been filled in, and the dumps of waste have long ago been hidden in Welforlands Fields, overgrown by dense shrubbery.

Although Shipton-under-Wychwood is in the forest area, it has a strong association with Cotswold and has one of the handsomest of all Cotswold mansions, described by one writer as 'a sermon of beauty through symmetry'. It stands near the highroad, and the passer-by catches a glimpse of it so that it haunts the mind like a dream building. The elegant stable block, however, can be seen from the road more clearly and is fine enough for any king's horses or his men. There is also the Shaven Crown Inn, a splendid example of enriched Cotswold vernacular said to have been built for the Abbey of Bruerne.

Shipton-under-Wychwood is also the home of the Groves family, who have been quarrymen, masons, carpenters and blacksmiths and have worked in all other crafts associated with iron, stone and timber for the past two hundred years or more. One member of the family, William Groves, worked for Christopher Wren as carpenter on the London churches after the Fire of London, and a pair of compasses and a bevel belonging to him are kept by the family. His son, John Groves, who died in 1761 and is buried in Shipton's churchyard, is said to have built the Shipton Court stables.

Yet another association Wychwood has with Cotswold is Cornbury, the mansion whose handsome front was designed and built by Timothy Strong and his son Valentine, masons of the Burford area who owned quarries in Taynton and Little Barrington that are renowned for the fine quality and golden colour of their stone. Valentine also began Park House at Fairford, but died before it was finished. His table tomb is in Fairford churchyard near the south porch. His name and year of death and the word 'freemason' are on a panel let into the side, and a panel now missing bore these words:

> Here's one that was an able workman long
> Who divers houses built, both fair and Strong;
> Though Strong he was, a Stronger came than he
> And robbed him of his Fame and Life, we see;

Moving an old house a new one for to rear
Death met him by the way and laid him here.

Some years ago, according to a leaflet issued by the Tolsey Museum, Burford, when the front of Cornbury Park was being renovated, the mason's marks of the men who carved the cornices were found still as fresh as when they were new, and it was possible in some cases to trace the families of a number of the men who worked on the mansion under Timothy Strong.

5 · Hampnett to Southrop

One of the pleasantest ways to the source of the Leach is to take the minor road that leaves the Foss just before the Northleach junction with the A40 and go off into the wolds above Prison Copse until one comes to Hampnett, where the springs of its rising can be seen on the sloping village green.

I like to go there in early autumn, for then the walker is generally accompanied by mixed flocks of linnets and goldfinches who dip and rise above the drystone walls in happy undulation while the breeze takes their chattering tinkling notes and tosses them around in the same manner as they toss the coloured leaves of maple and hawthorn floating from the bushes growing along the wayside. The birds, pursuing some migratory course known only to themselves, are journeying without urgency; there is still plenty of food, mellow sunshine to warm a cool breeze, and winter yet a couple of months away. Also early autumn is a good time of the year for the upland scene, for the sun turns the predominating yellow tones to gold, and the stubble, the hawkweeds, mulleins, yellow toadflax, kexes and drying grasses of the wayside all take on this golden glow on the right kind of day.

Birds come to mind when I think of Hampnett – not living birds but those carved on the choir-arch of the little Norman church, one pair of doves drinking from a bowl neck to neck and another pair breast to breast, with nothing grotesque in the carving as in most Norman work for these are gentle creatures of simple, plump, rounded shapes. They stand out because they were outlined in black paint in a re-decorating of the whole of the chancel by Messrs Clay & Bell and the rector, Mr Wiggins, in the 1840s, medieval church painting being Mr Wiggins' hobby. The Reverend Francis Witt noted in his diary on 20 September 1848 that Mr Wiggins was assisting the Rector of Stow in 'enriching the chancel by painting the sedilla a rich blue colour with the sacred monogram and stars picked out in gold . . . Mr Wiggins, whose taste leads him in the lines of medieval architecture and church decoration'. I get the impression that Francis Witt did not quite see the necessity of reviving this form of decoration. Another contemporary wrote that, 'It was decked and bedizened like a fairground.' The general opinion is that the effect is pleasing, though perhaps there is a little too much of it. The first time the congregation of Hampnett saw it in all its glory, they must have been filled with wonder, but as, on the whole, church congregations tend to be conservative, they probably preferred the old grey interior of their church and found it hard to believe Mr Wiggins when he told them that for some two hundred years after the church was built its walls had been adorned with coloured pictures.

Hampnett used to be on the route of the famous Flyer coaches, but in the late eighteenth century the roads in the Leach valley in the vicinity of Northleach were particularly atrocious, so the coaches took the ancient green road that kept to the hills north of the town and that went past Hampnett village. The eighteenth-century traveller and writer, Arthur Young, complained bitterly of the way the road had been mended by filling in the ruts with loose stones 'as large as one's head' bringing to mind those lanes described by Jorrocks as 'deeply spur-lingered, clayey-bottomed'. When the turnpike had been improved, the coaches were re-routed through Northleach, bringing sorely needed custom to the little town.

The Leach comes down from Hampnett, still only a trickle, to begin its journey to the Thames at Lechlade. It is fed by springs in the marshy ground by the old prison at Northleach, giving off 'foul miasmas' as one writer of the period called them and affecting the unfortunate occupants already suffering from damp walls and floors and other miseries. The number of prisoners dying of jail fever in Northleach far exceeded those in other prisons, many dying before they were tried and convicted. In the late eighteenth century Sir Onesipherus Paul, son of a wealthy Woodchester clothier, became interested in prison reform, the conditions and the attitude to prisoners at that time being so inhumane that his declaration 'Bread, water, and air as a means of a healthy existence should be denied to no prisoner', made in 1783, was considered a revolutionary statement of prison reform. He did not cease to work for this until he died in 1820, writing many treatises on the subject in the high-falutin style of the period. I doubt if anyone except a student of the subject would have the patience to read them today, but they did help to change the terrible conditions of the prisons at that time.

With or without his approval, the prisoners were put to work on a treadwheel. In 1827 the Reverend Francis Witt in his duty as magistrate inspected the treadwheel installed at Northleach Brideswell and wrote that the machinery still required attention. The velocity with which the wheel revolved was too great, so that it exceeded the strength of the prisoners. Although the treadwheel was used to grind corn, it was kept working as part of the punishment even when there was no corn to be ground. Each man worked for about five minutes at a time, while a relay of men was kept in an adjacent yard walking in a circle. This soul-destroying form of punishment seemed to provoke no compassion in the mind of the rector, beyond his calling them 'miserable wretches'. The old prison is now a county museum, but some of its exhibits keep the barbarities of the nineteenth century in mind.

The golden age of Northleach was in the days of the wool trade, when its church was rebuilt in the Perpendicular style by the wealthy wool-men whose memorial brasses survive in the church as evidence of their gifts and occupation. Whereas other Cotswold churches were rebuilt by one or two wool-men, Northleach had half a dozen such patrons, including John Fortey, who built the nave, and Will Midwinter, the most important factor in the town, whose brass lies at the foot of the pulpit.

The oldest of the memorial brasses to a wool-man and his wife, dated about 1400, is supposed to have come from the original church before its rebuilding. The memorials reveal the life of those times as in a picturebook. The brass of Thomas Bushe, for instance, who died in 1525, and his wife, both wearing the dress of the period: Thomas is in a fur-trimmed mantle, his wife in a tight-fitting gown with long, full skirts. The wool-men had their brasses made in the Low Countries before they died, and Thomas Bushe was determined to let the world know he was a wool-merchant, for in the spandrels of the canopy over the effigies are engraved curly horned sheep, a large bush, evidently a rebus, and the arms of the Staple of Calais of which he was a member. His merchant's mark, a monogram with a cross ascending from it, is placed beneath the two figures, and their feet rest on a woolsack and a sheep. But he showed the world he was not proud in death, for a humble inscription 'Off yr Charitie P'y for the

Northleach porch and Kitty Midwinter's tombstone

40

TO THE MEMORIE
KITTY WIFE OF
JOSEPH MIDWINTER
DIED JUNE 9 1858
Aged 78 Years

soulle of Thomas Bushe and his wife' is inscribed between two decorated pillars framing the effigies.

Another, smaller brass belongs to Robert Serche, who died in 1501, his wife and four children. Robert has long, straight hair, and his gown has a fur-trimmed collar and fur-lined sleeves. A monogram of the initials R and A entwined together in a roundel is placed above the effigies, and these do not show the couple looking upwards like most such figures but have the heads turned a little towards each other, suggesting a delightful intimacy in death as in life. There is also a memorial to a vicar of the church, who died about 1530, the inscription giving a gloomy warning that death may come when it is least expected. Perhaps he had a premonition that the wool trade was coming to an end, and with it Northleach's prosperous years.

We know about Will Midwinter not only from his brass but from the Cely letters written between 1475 and 1488, delightfully human documents written by members of the family to each other and including intimate details about their private as well as their business lives. The Cely family shared the work: one was captain of their ship, transporting the wool to the Low Countries and as much at home there as in England; another looked after the London warehouse, and George spent his time travelling the Cotswolds buying wool from the sheep-farmers as well as from Will Midwinter, riding with his hawk on his wrist to provide his dinner and to relieve the tedium of lonely journeys. They frequently disagreed with Will Midwinter's prices, but it could have been a form of bargaining, for they continued to trade with him despite their bitter comments on his charges. In the churchyard there is a headstone to a Kitty Midwinter who died in 1858, and the name appears frequently in parish records from 1586 until today.

The chief glory of Northleach church is its south porch, and whenever I see it, I get the same warm glow of appreciation of the masons' skill. I still keep in my memory a small incident that happened many years ago. I was looking up at the pinnacles and crockets to see if I could recognize the chimney belonging to the fireplace of the upper room in the porch when an elderly verger spoke to me and I told him what I was doing. He told me to watch the top of a buttress in the centre of the west side and then disappeared, and in a few moments I saw a wavering plume of white smoke ascending to the sky above one of the pinnacles. The chimney had been artfully concealed so as not to spoil the symmetry of the design. The verger came to me beaming with delight, rather like an amateur wizard who has successfully produced his best party-piece of magic, and although I suspected he had done it before and kept a supply of dried sticks for the purpose, he was as gratified by my response as I was by this kindly, amusing act.

The church and buildings of the same date as the church are of a fine-quality stone dug out of the 'Guggle', a stone-mine at the far end of the village. The Guggle mine, named after a pub, was discovered accidentally. A new subsidence on a spot where a woman usually stood her pram with a baby in it caused it to be opened up and a tunnel was found. The mine level ran for some two hundred yards, and tradition says that during the Civil Wars the stained glass from the church windows was hidden there. There used to be bizarre stories told about this tunnel – tunnels always stimulated country people's imaginations – and a particularly interesting one says that a gold coffin has been buried at the end of it, suggesting the story-tellers mixed up old folklore concerning long barrows and other large artificial mounds such as Silbury Hill in Wiltshire where it was said a knight in golden armour had been buried.

Some of the masons who worked on the church have left their marks, and to those fascinated by the craft of Cotswold masonry these can be as moving as names on headstones turning abstractions into people. In most cases the marking was to let the master mason know who had done a particular piece of work, but the words scratched on the south-east column of the nave arcade, 'Henrie Winchcombe God grant us his grace', were probably graffiti and not a true mark. There were many of the name in the district, including a famous wool-man, and a Richard Winchcombe was a master mason in the first half of the fifteenth century; we know he travelled to Taynton to purchase stone for the building of New College, Oxford, his expenses for the journey being entered into the accounts, which have come down to us. David Verey suggests the whole family may have originated in the Windrush-Taynton quarry areas where some of the best stone on Cotswold was quarried and mined, the tradition of good masonry continuing long after the masons of the Burford area who helped Sir Christopher Wren build St Paul's and other London churches died out. A stone-carver of great skill must have been responsible for the stone pulpit, one of the few in Gloucestershire with the elegant fluted trumpet stem.

The Northleach Wolds, an area of sheep-walks in the fifteenth and sixteenth centuries, were well known to Will Midwinter and the Cely family, for it was from them that wool was collected and then sent to London and on to the Continent. Wool was so profitable that sheep-walks replaced other forms of farms, and the villages were often reduced to the few cottages needed to house the shepherds. Even today one gets a sense of remoteness on these hills with the sky dominating the landscape and the ancient burial mounds signposting the Salt Way and other trackways that seem to be pointing back to the Middle Ages and into prehistory rather than forward into habitations of today.

Notgrove, that quiet and private place, has its church, manor-house and complex of farm buildings grouped together, and going to the church by a short by-lane one has the feeling of trespassing. The church is said to have been built on the site of a Roman burial ground, but the Saxon origin is more evident because of the small, battered sculpture of the Crucifixion set in a decorated niche on the outside of the east wall, suggesting a Saxon church on the site. The carving is far more appealing in its crude simplicity than more elaborate work of later times; there is so little to get between the piety of the sculptor and his material.

Two effigies of fourteenth-century priests that were once in the churchyard have been brought inside, showing up the pitted, weathered stone. The economical carving of the long lines of the folds of the robes is still well defined and has a venerable austerity due to age and the excellent flowing lines of the carvings. There are also three freestone effigies of members of the Whittington family who owned the manor from 1587 to 1630, but they do not show the same strict artistry. A modern tapestry designed by Colin Skelton and worked by him and his family, completed in 1954 and used as a reredos, brings warmth into the little church, and in future years this will be a treasure more widely recognized, for there is history as well as skill in the design.

Turkdean, about two miles south of Notgrove, is a little oasis in the dry wolds, with its splendid avenue of beeches marching up to the village from Lower Dean where in spring one can find marsh marigolds and drifts of cuckoo flowers spangling the water-meadows not far from an old manor-house with gables and Tudor windows.

Aldsworth, on the fringe of the wolds, was the home of Shepherd Wilcox who looked after the last prize flock of the old Cotswold sheep, the 'lions' with their curly forelocks, the distinguishing mark of the breed. They should also have 'long, level and broad backs, slightly overhanging rumps, tall enough to look over the hurdles, fleece open and curly, sometimes exceeding fourteen pounds, and

Beech avenue below Turkdean

clean white legs', according to the official description. They can be seen today in the Cotswold Farm Park near Guiting, with other rare breeds. I remember seeing the flock many years ago and watching the shepherd preparing a sheep for show. Having carefully trimmed the forelock, he tied it with a piece of blue ribbon to keep it out of the way while he finished the long face, and he chuckled with me to see it thus adorned. The sheep tossed her head as if she were indignant that I had laughed at her, and I felt quite guilty at having done so. I apologized to her but it is difficult to reach any rapport with a sheep unless one is a shepherd.

Continuing its journey from Northleach, the river flows past Upper End and Eastington through Dodge Park and goes winding along

45

View of Akeman Street crossing Leach valley with Cotswold Lions

through fields and woods unknown except by the few who live near it, for there are no footpaths along its banks. It comes into its own as a delightful little Cotswold river and for this part of its journey is as clear and sparkling as the Coln or Windrush. It runs between Eastleach Martin and Eastleach Turville, where a large, flat stone bridge joins the two villages. An ancient church with a bellcote stands in a grassy churchyard; on the other side is the ancient church of St Andrew in Eastleach Turville, with a fine Norman doorway whose tympanum is said to be in the same vibrant style as the one at Quenington, showing a carving of Christ in Majesty. The reason for the two churches is that there were two manors held by two different lords, and each must have his church. The Keble family were lords of the manor in the sixteenth century, and the family again became prominent when John Keble, author of *The Christian Year* (1827), became curate. This was how the footbridge that makes such a picturesque addition to the village became known as Keble's Bridge. In spring the river banks are lined with daffodils, the yellow trumpets making a splendid foil to lichened stone and clear blue water. The daffodils have spread in recent years in gatherings and clumps from the river banks to wherever they can find a space on the two levels holding the cottages and houses.

When I go to the Eastleach villages in spring to look at the daffodils, I take the opportunity of visiting George Swinford, an old friend of Freda Derrick, whose book *Cotswold Stone* is still one of the most enlightening on the subject. Even at ninety-seven, George Swinford, quarryman, mason, tiler, raconteur on all things Cotswold, kindly host and keeper of his own little museum at Filkins, can still warm to the subject of Cotswold stone with a sparkle in his eye and voice. His little museum contains bygones he has collected himself locally from people he knew, and he can still tell the story of them all and how he came to find them, bringing back the hardships and pleasures of village life nearly a hundred years ago. Sir Stafford Cripps, once Chancellor of the Exchequer, who owned much of the village, gave him the job of reroofing the village, which was in dis-repair, and of building a group of new houses in the vernacular. George did the job from top to bottom, one might say, because first he had to dig the stone from the quarries in the field, then shape the slates and finally put them on the roofs, and a very good job he made of it. He was Sir Stafford Cripps' foreman in all the improvements he made in the village, including many lengths of good stone walling and the introduction of 'planks', thin sheets of stone that were

Clapper bridge to Eastleach Martin Church

fastened by iron ties made by the local blacksmith; looking not unlike
the headstones arranged side by side to enclose gardens, they are a
characteristic of Filkins. George explained how these rectangles of
stone could be used to build pigsties, and in his time, when every
cottager kept a pig, he had made many of them, shaping the stone
to hold rough rafters for the roofs. When I spoke to him recently, he
was annoyed that many people had been breaking up the 'planks'
for stone for crazy paving for which they could get a good price.
'Anywhere you dig, there's stone under the ground waiting to be
used,' he told me, and he went on to make a map showing the places
in and around Filkins where there were different types of oolite useful
for different purposes.

Herringbone masonry in N and S walls of nave, Southrop Church

49

Old cottages and stone plank fencing, Filkins

George also wrote a history of his life, a valuable document for historians studying the late nineteenth and early twentieth centuries, and a human document as well, for it tells of a life of long hours of work from when he was ten years old to when he retired – and his retirement was later than that of most workers. An Oxford library has his autobiography, and he has also recorded some of his experiences as local mason and tiler; future generations, hearing the rich voice with its suggestion of a humorous chuckle in it, should be able to identify not only with George Swinford master mason but with the medieval masons who like him began as a quarryman and learnt to know the fabric they worked with from the moment it came out of the ground into the light of day. As Freda Derrick once said about such Cotsallers, 'For them the stone is in the blood.'

The Leach comes to Southrop on its last few miles, before, within sight of Lechlade, it empties itself into the Thames. At Southrop it

George Swinford's Council cottages, Filkins

makes an attractive water-garden for the manor-house not far from where the ancient church stands half hidden by massive barns. There was once a Saxon church on the site but the big patch of herringbone masonry, the largest and best example of Cotswold of this form of walling, is said to be of later date, belonging to the north doorway with its Norman arch and diapered tympanum. The Knights Hospitallers of St John's of Clerkenwell, London, owned it in the thirteenth century.

Its famous font, dated 1180, was discovered by John Keble when he was curate of Southrop in 1823–5, and though it did not accord with his kind of Christianity, he had the understanding to keep it in the church. For those who can interpret the symbolism, it is a complete scripture lesson from the Old Testament. The bowl is divided into eight arches, five showing Virtues in the form of female warriors trampling on their opposite Vices, seen as hideous, squirm-

51

ing figures under their feet. It is far removed from the naïve Christianity of the Saxons and the crude grotesques of the later Normans, a sophisticated exposition of Good and Evil practically meaningless except to students of theology. A young friend who was with me one time said, 'It doesn't look English!' and that, I think is the explanation. The Christian religion in those days was not a native product but one enriched with art and ideas from the Continent and from the East.

6 · Broadway and the Villages of the Edge

Broadway at the beginning of the century was one of the villages chosen by people sufficiently attracted by the charm and distinction of Cotswold to want to live there. And it was at this time that the regeneration of the village began, for it had sadly deteriorated during the depressions of the late nineteenth century and the loss of its coach trade, many of its larger ancient mansions falling into decay or being made into tenements for poor people, and in one case made into a workhouse.

The village today still keeps a few buildings dating from the late sixteenth century but most of the picturesque cottages and houses are of a much later date, and one architect assured me that at least half of them were Victorian, but he, I think, looked on the village with a jaundiced eye, saying it had surrendered itself to commercialism. Many people take this view, not understanding that its position makes it easily accessible from the industrial Midlands and that it has always been a town for travellers seeking rest and refreshment. True, it can be uncomfortably full in the season, though since the new Leisure Park on Broadway Hill was opened the crowds are moving up the hill where there is ample space for everyone. For my part the good Guiting stone used for most of its buildings gives Broadway a pleasant unity whatever their date, and if the street is not too packed with parked cars and rambling visitors, the spaciousness of its broad way gives it dignity and grace.

There is nothing poky or small about Broadway, for unlike many Cotswold villages it is not squeezed into a narrow valley but has room to expand. Thomas Babington wrote in his *Survey of Worcestershire*: 'Broadweye, the broad and highe waye from the Shepherdes Cottes which on the mounted woldes shelter themselfes under hylls from the rage of storme down to the most fruitful Vale of Eusham . . . is a town extended in a street tedyous in lengthe, especially in winter.'

This street 'tedyous in lengthe' once had twenty-three inns to make it less tedious on the long walk from one end to the other and to serve the many travellers who used it as a stopping place for the night in their journeys through the county.

According to an 'Examplicication of a Decree' relating to Broadway in 1422, the main road came down from the top by Conigree Lane, entering the village opposite the old church at Bury End, which was the site of the original village about a mile from the main road of today. Two hundred years later, in the *Britannia* of 1675, Ogilvy states that the road came down Fish Hill but at the bottom turned left through West End to go to Worcester as the old road had done.

As soon as the main road up Fish Hill was well established, a new village began to grow up along it, the old village became isolated, Conigree Lane became the private drive of Middle Hill, and St Eadburgha's became too far out of the village to be easily accessible, so a new church, St Michael's was built nearer the village on the site of an old chapel of ease. Deserted St Eadburgha's mouldered away, but now, after years of neglect, it has been renovated. In the summer there are services in the church, in the winter it is kept open, and it is cherished all the year round. It has one of the most peaceful churchyards I know, sloping down gently to a little tributary of the Avon with moorhens walking about the tombs, and blackbirds, thrushes, wrens, robins and many other birds finding sanctuary there. It has a good mounting block and stone steps by the church yard wall, the whole delightful corner overhung by trees.

Not far from the church on the way to the village there is a gateway, all that remains of Court House, once the home of Anthony Daston and his second wife, Anne Savage, who had been born a Sheldon and whose first husband was a Savage of Elmley Castle. There is a brass to Anthony Daston in the church on the west wall, showing him wearing a breastplate and shirt of mail, his helmet under his head. Anne Daston was 'the most bountiful gentlewoman for hospitality of her degree in England', according to Babington. The Sheldons were a family famous for tapestry-weaving at Barcheston and who owned much property in Warwickshire and elsewhere; Broadway came into their possession in 1575, and they remained lords of the manor until 1675. The Sheldons were Royalists, and it is said that, when King Charles was on his way to Evesham on

St Eadburgha's church, Broadway

12 May 1645, he stayed with a Sheldon at Broadway Court and that
it was on that night that the flames of Campden House, set alight to
save it falling into the hands of the Parliamentarians, lit up Broadway Hill as Prince Rupert marched with his rearguard after the
King.

Shakespeare must have known the hospitality of Anne Daston.
The latest additions to his saga prove an extension of his social life,
for it has been difficult to believe that his circle of acquaintances
was limited to the townspeople of Stratford-upon-Avon and the
immediate neighbourhood. E. A. Barnard, in *New Links with Shakespeare* shows that Shakespeare's acquaintances extended to Chipping
Campden and Broadway and that he was linked by a network of
blood and marriage relationships with the Combe family.

A place of meeting was the Great Farm, Broadway, where Anne
Daston lived after she was widowed until she died in 1619, and her
sons by her first marriage who looked after the farm were cousins of
Thomas and William Coombe – Shakespeare left his sword to
Thomas Coombe of the College, Stratford-upon-Avon. Henry Sturley, son of Shakespeare's intimate friend and solicitor Abraham
Sturley, was vicar of Broadway from 1610 to 1639, and this must
have been another connection with Broadway. He may even have
attended services at St Eadburgha's, for in those days it was custom-
ary for friends to sleep where they dined because of the hazards of
night travel. It is pleasing to think of him, after the long pull up to
Mickleton, riding along the top to come to Conigree Lane and then
down the steepish track to Bury End and the welcome hospitality of
the 'most bounteous gentlewoman of her degree in the neighbourhood'.

South of Broadway are the villages of Buckland, Laverton, Stanton
and Stanway, lying in narrow valleys coming down from the Edge
and reached by footpaths and minor roads. Buckland, about a mile
from Broadway, has its houses and cottages most cunningly sited
amongst little humps and hollows below the escarpment in a picturesque disarray of groups of trees, and it looks sheltered, secluded
without being remote. It had associations with William Morris, who
restored the sixteenth-century glass in the church at his own expense
lest it become lost through neglect. There are two carved stones with
recessed panels showing an angel in each, most delicately painted in
pure colour faded with time but still recognizable as angels of the
reassuring not the avenging kind; they are supposed to have come

Wainscotting with hat-pegs, Buckland

from Hailes at the Dissolution, as well as the embroidered cope made with pieces of vestments that have borders of pomegranates, the emblem of Katherine of Aragon. The frailty of age reveals rather than diminishes the quality of the embroidery, for this is English embroidery at its most exquisite, excelling any produced on the Continent at that time. It was the way the great ladies in their castles and fortified manor-houses spent many of the long hours while their lords and masters were away at the wars, at Court or out hunting, and many longings and fears must have been stitched into their work.

The church also has some oak wainscoting with hat-pegs, and this has survived since 1615, though Atkyns, in his *History of Gloucestershire*, says Sir John Thynne of Longleat (1557) was responsible for it. The lasting qualities of English oak would seem to be almost as long as stone if not attacked by beetle.

Laverton lies less than a mile south-west of Buckland. Here Mary Osborne taught the village women to spin and weave so they might have the pleasure of learning a craft outside their usual domestic occupations. An elderly woman once showed me with pride a piece of cloth she had woven there after collecting the wool sheep had left on the hedgerows, spinning it and then weaving the yarn. She told me fourteen women once turned their spinning-wheels together in that tiny cottage, in days when it was the custom of the men to spend their evenings in the pub, and the women had nowhere to go and must stay at home.

After much endeavour Mary Osborne achieved her centre where village life could be invigorated by the teaching of handicrafts and association with artists, master craftsmen, musicians and others of like mind. It was a noble project, and though village life is much less restricted nowadays because of radio, television and the new interests the retired incomers have brought to the villages, the Guild House stands out bravely on the hillside, a beacon showing the way to creative experiences for the villages around.

Many of the smaller villages are no longer inhabited by those earning a living on the land but by retired gentlefolk and wealthy commuters who cherish the Cotswold vernacular to excess but, unlike the local gentry who belong to the place by birth or ancestry, feel no more than an aesthetic attachment to it. The natives who remain regard the new residents with unsympathatic curiosity on the whole and even occasionally with malignant glee when they get into trouble because of their lack of understanding of local conditions and view the new tidiness, the neat garden hedges and mown grass verges, with unease. But while the natives feel with every fibre of their being that the village belongs to those born and bred in the place as well as the dead in the churchyard, most have never consciously attempted to improve its appearance and have often injured its comeliness through ignorance, indifference or sheer bloodymindedness – and the newcomers' efforts make them realize this.

But the new residents are not a stable population, having no roots in the place, and the delights of the countryside can grow less as they grow older. While they can sell at a profit and move to a place with urban amenities, the village loses its character and continuity as the population changes. But though the village in the old sense has come to an end, it is a better end than one of squalid decay. One realizes this coming upon a derelict hamlet and group of roofless farm buildings fallen into decay such as that at Far Upton Wold near Blockley where, in a wide upland landscape of huge fields, the remains of such a lost complex huddled together in a shallow fold on the hilltop tell their own melancholy story of the end of the old kind of farming and the triumph of the new, with manpower reduced to the minimum.

Holiday self-catering cottages are multiplying on Cotswold, so one wonders at times if in a few years there will not be enough of the genuine villages to make it worth while for people to visit them. Buckland and Laverton have their share and with admirable taste preserve the vernacular, but the life has gone out of it, and it has become a mockery of itself. True, the people holiday cottages attract are usually country-lovers who enjoy living in a charming fairy-tale cottage perhaps with a stream at its door, wooded hills and grassy slopes as backcloth, but they contribute little to the village and leave the place denuded of residents in the winter. As one old-embittered resident told me: 'They comes and they goes like the cuckoo and the swallows, fairweather birds.' Moreover, the firms or individuals who buy up, restore and furnish the cottages are seldom local people but outsiders taking advantage of the market for first-class holiday accommodation. It is the most secluded, most picturesque villages, those most loved by Cotswold enthusiasts all the world over, that are losing their identity in this way. The smallest villages are particularly vulnerable.

I was looking over a restored stretch of dry-stone walling into a cottage garden and idly wondering why the grass plot and a few shrubs looked tidy but unloved when an old man came and stood by my side. He gave me a polite greeting and I could see by the gleam in his eye he wanted an audience. A vintage village ancient, a rarity in these days, I told myself. Knowing this was a village where there were many holiday cottages with an old manor-house turned into a hotel (where every oak beam and copper hunting horn added a few more dollars to the bill) I wondered, not too seriously, if the old man had been imported to add a little rusticity to the scene in the way landowners in the eighteenth century paid a hermit to occupy a false hermitage on their estates as part of the romantic trimmings, but I soon discovered he was a genuine native. After a preliminary skirmish, when he tried to find out where I came from, who I was and what I was doing in his village, I discovered he was a native with a grievance he wanted to talk about. He resented the way old cottages had been made into holiday homes. I pointed out how skilfully they had been modernized. They improved the village, I said, purposely provoking him.

'Even if I'd never seen 'un before, I could tell what they was,' he told me and went on to say that the owner of the holiday cottages made more money in the summer months than the farmer did from his barley, pigs and milk after working all the year round seven days a week. 'It's one of them companies,' he added darkly, looking at me from under his bushy eyebrows to see if I understood how the unholy workings of high finance had penetrated the village.

'But how can you tell a holiday cottage from any other?' I asked him.

'By the gardens, of course. Folks as lives here proper must have taters and greens and such tack. And where's the shed for their tools, their onions and sacks of taters for the winter? Village folk wouldn't waste good ground like that,' and he pointed to the grass plot contemptuously. 'Good ground it is too. I knew the old couple who lived there – grew a couple of bags of taters as well as greens. Break his heart to see it now.'

His grand-daughter came and herded him away, a bossy little woman but kindly, proud of him in her own way. 'He's ninety and still does the garden, but he does go on so,' she said apologetically.

'He taught me something I should have realized myself,' I told her.

'We old 'uns ain't all daft,' he said with an emphasis on the word 'old' and a malicious twinkle in his eye as she led him away.

'Grampy, how could you?' I heard her say, and enjoyed his unrepentant chuckle, his reply of 'She's no chicken!'

Stanton, the largest of the four villages, begins in the Vale approached by roads overhung by chestnuts and oaks and ascends the hill in a long, winding street lined with handsome stone houses and cottages that appear to belong to the seventeenth century onward, the earliest bearing the dates of their origin, 1604, 1615, 1618. All are excellently restored and well kept, the aura of medievalism kept within the bounds of good taste.

When I am asked to show American visitors typical Cotswold village architecture, I take them to Stanton and if possible arrange it so that they see it when the evening light falls kindly upon the old stone and brings out the texture and hidden sunlight in the colour. The houses show the variations of dormers, round-headed Jacobean windows, mullions, drip-stones, labels and finials stonemasons could devise and which in Stanton mark a period of material prosperity of the yeoman farmers and merchants who lived there.

By the end of the nineteenth century, like much of Cotswold, Stanton was falling into decay, but as has happened before a man of wealth and understanding saved it from the pitiful makeshifts of the twentieth century and gave it the comeliness we see today. He was Philip Stott, of Oldham, later Sir Philip, who in 1906 began the work of repair, continuing for the next twenty years though interrupted during the 1914–18 war, when it had to be slowed down. He was a practical-minded man as well as a man of ideals and gave the village a water-supply, electricity, a village hall, street lamps and a bathing pool at the top of the village fed by the springs of Shenbarrow Hill. At the vale end of the village he set two ancient barns from elsewhere, one half-timbered, the other thatched, and it seemed right it should be so, not only because they give the village a handsome beginning at the lower end but because they point to the fact that the village begins in the well-wooded country of the Vale when in medieval days timber was the building material rather than stone; then, as it rises up into high country, the buildings are of stone in true Cotswold fashion. The barns have been made into dwellings today but a pair of wooden doors survive with a simple stout latch and bar in the Cotswold style that was once used for farm gates. Despite the aged, fibrous appearance of the wood, smooth with much handling, the doors are still as efficient as when they were first made. It is good to see the work of some unknown village carpenter still in use and not in a museum, for it is when the past survives to serve the present that we realize the value of the old skills.

From the ramparts of the Iron Age camp of Shenbarrow south-east

Didbrook and North Cerney. Two windows commemorating Abbot Whitchurch

of the village, Stanton has one of the best Cotswold view-points I know. On a clear day one can see Langley earthworks, Nottingham and Oxenton Hills, as the Iron Age men who used Shenbarrow must have done. And if one is a little weary after the climb, there is a pub perched on a knoll where the traveller can find refreshment.

Stanway today consists of a mansion, Stanway House, with its superb gatehouse, its tithe barn built to hold the corn and wool of Tewkesbury Abbey which originally held the manor, St Peter's Church, the Old Vicarage, the Old Bakehouse, a few scattered cottages and a magnificent view-point through gaps in the beech-woods where the turnpike, now the B4077, descends Stanway Hill.

The gatehouse and the tithe barn are at two ends of an architectural scale, the gatehouse ornate, flamboyant, proclaiming the Tracys'

62

ancestry with every cockleshell aloft and the long, low barn fitting into the background as if it had grown out of the earth like the ancient trees about it. It is now the village hall and has come to a good use now its days as a barn are over. The church is disappointing: the crude yellow ochre of its stone does not fit well into its surroundings, and one would expect some good tombs in the churchyard and more affinity with the mansion. Perhaps, being near a crossroads that lead down into the Vale, it suffered during the Civil Wars and has never recovered, while a restoration in 1896 reduced it still further.

The Tracy family acquired the manor in the sixteenth century from Tewkesbury Abbey, and from the Tracy family it came to the Earl of Wemyss. The front of the mansion presents an unbroken range of triple mullioned and transomed windows, pairs between each of the three gables with the bay window under the fourth gable. The south front has two storeys and a pierced parapet, the entrance with pilasters and a pediment of 1724 with the arms of the Tracy and Atkyns side by side similar to those on the gatehouse.

The gatehouse, of three storeys providing lodges with bay windows, is set at right angles to the house and church and is the most arresting feature of the group. It used to be said that Inigo Jones (1573–1652) designed it, and from its appearance it might well have been so, but it is now thought to have been designed by Timothy Strong, of the family of master masons who did much work on the new St Paul's after the Fire of London in 1666 and on other country houses, including Cornbury Park. If so, then the arms of Tracy and Atkyn displayed in the centre must have been added later. The noble archway is flanked by fluted columns standing on plinths, and there is a high garden wall protecting the south front with oval windows, though these are placed too high to see through without climbing up. They break the large, plain surface so that the wall is not forbidding but part of the grandeur of the entrance.

The tithe barn, built some two or three hundred years before the mansion, has a stone roof, and inside massive roof timbers give the impression of enormous strength and power.

The war memorial, at the corner of the crossroads, a bronze of St George and the Dragon by Alexander Fisher, is set on a stone plinth, and the lettering is by Eric Gill. The figure stands lithe as a ballet dancer poised delicately as he thrusts his spear into the dragon at his feet.

Captain Robert Dover of Dover's Games was buried in Stanway,

Granary on staddle-stones beside the Cotswold Way above Wood Stanway

though he has no monument or any inscription on his grave. The poet Michael Drayton in 1636 wrote in *Annalia Dubrensis*, a collection of mediocre poems about the games:

> We'll have thy statue in some rock cut out,
> With brave inscriptions garnished about
> And underwritten – Lo! this is the man
> Dover, that first those noble sports began.

But poets are notoriously fickle, and it was not until some three hundred years later that there was a memorial to him – and that a small one, on Dover's Hill above Chipping Campden where the games took place. After being abolished in 1852, the games were

Stanway gatehouse

restored as a tourist attraction, and in a different form in 1934, the old ferocious combats including shin-kicking not taking place, for these sports have been known to cripple a combatant for life. The most delightful and picturesque part of the Dover's Hill Games is the torchlight procession winding down the hill to the town as darkness falls and looking like a medieval procession of pilgrims as, wrapped and hooded against the cold, the company make their way in the flickering torchlight.

7 · *Chipping Campden and Border Villages*

Many hundreds of thousands of words have been written about Chipping Campden, and many more photographs taken of its church, almshouses and market hall, while the drawings, paintings and woodcuts having Campden as the subject must be legion. It has still the same irresistible appeal it had in the early 1900s, when its charm and beauty were praised by visiting poets and essayists who, though not aware of it at the time, gave Campden a publicity that makes it possible for the town to live mainly by its tourist trade today.

Others who have rescued it from decay and depressions through the centuries include William Grevel, the wool-man, who left money in his will to help build the church and whose fourteenth-century house still survives with its bay window of two storey and six lights; a traceried panel in between and gargoyles above arrest the eye not only because of their obvious antiquity but for the distinction they bring to that end of the High Street. Wherever one looks in Campden, there are seventeenth- and eighteenth-century features, and the little town, in well-bred fashion, is aware of its distinction.

Sir Baptist Hicks was another benefactor who enriched both town and church through his help with building the group consisting of the church, the Jacobean gateway of the magnificent manor-house destroyed during the Civil War, the almshouses dating from about 1612 perched above the road with their gables, bays, two storeys and four-centred arched doorways. This collection is one of the best examples of the Cotswold domestic style.

Much later came C. R. Ashbee, the architect and craftsman who in 1902 brought his Guild of Craftsmen from the East End of London in an attempt to help his craftsmen and bring new life to the town, which was much decayed. Brian Smith, the Gloucestershire archivist, discovered hundreds of Poor Law Papers in the Record Office showing how desperately poor the citizens of Chipping Campden

Chipping Campden wool church and gatehouse to the manor

had been for the past two hundred years. Although the Guild wound up in 1909, it helped repopulate Campden and rejuvenate it, for the town had become, in a modest way, a centre for arts and crafts, a refuge, because of its evasive charms, from the harsh industrial world elsewhere. A Campden Trust was formed 'to promote the reputation of the town as an art centre', and its aims also included the restoration and care of Campden's old buildings and keeping the town free from eyesores that might spoil its harmony. As Professor Finberg once said of Campden and Northleach, 'They have the nature of rare survival.'

I like to come to Campden from high Cotswold, dropping down into the town after passing Kiftsgate Stone where it lies hidden in wayside jungle. The stone is said to mark one of the boundaries of the Hundred of Kiftsgate to which Campden belongs. The road on which it stands being on the site of an ancient trackway, it may well be so, for trackways or Roman roads were often used as boundary landmarks, but local historians today keep silent about the stone's authenticity. The spot stays in my mind because it was here, under the wayside shrubs, that we used to pick the first wild sweet violets of the year in the Easter holidays years ago. But last year when I went to look for the stone only a few ragged plants remained to show the way to it.

As the road begins to descend, one can see Campden in its long, wide valley enfolded in a gap between lesser hills, its church tower standing out amongst trees sometimes grey and unsubstantial as mist or ivory-pale in an illuminating light. Sometimes villages that look enchanting from the hills prove disappointing on closer acquaintance, but Campden does not disappoint in this way. Early morning or late evening is the best time to stand and stare at it – safer also, for traffic can be heavy in the High Street in the season. Then the wide High Street comes into its own and one feels the old magic of the long, curving High Street fading away into the Vale and knows it is still there if one is willing to accept it.

In the twelfth century the ancient track, a fork of the White Way, was known as 'the track leading from Cirencester to Campden'; therefore, when Hugh de Gondeville established a borough and a market here in the 1280s, there was already through traffic going north and south. After going through the town, the track descended the scarp and led directly through Mickleton to Stratford-on-Avon. This market was the beginning of Campden as a town of some importance, for it was not only a place for the buying and selling of wool but one where local people could spend the money they had earned by sheep-rearing on goods brought in by traders that could not be bought at home. It was not only the big sheep-farmers who had fleeces to sell; many of the peasants reared a few sheep on common land to make a little extra money.

Though it has kept much of its old unity of appearance, there have been many changes in Campden since the last world war. When I knew it in the 1920s, one could walk along the High Street on a summer evening and chat to the old men in their shirtsleeves smoking their pipes and sitting at their cottage doors enjoying the last of the evening sun. The cottages themselves were more primitive in their amenities. Today, externally, except for an unmistakable air of belonging to the kind of people who would never sit in their doorways in shirtsleeves smoking shag, the cottages keep their simple, sturdy shapes, self-consciously, perhaps, but not outrageously gentrified. It is the type of inhabitants who have changed. Some are holiday visitors who have hired a cottage for a week or two; others are occupied by retired gentlefolk who for the most part are delighted to live in such a charming place.

At times I regret the loss of the old alleys between the shops and houses in the High Street where one caught glimpses of narrow gardens, miniscule cottages and back yards hung with washing and littered with buckets, brooms, dog kennels and strings of onions hanging on the walls because the people who lived there never had enough room in their cottages for these things. The entrances to the alleys, where they still exist, have doors to them now, and there are no more of those intimate glimpses of back-alley life – even Poppet's Alley, so called because a woman fond of finery and nicknamed 'Lady Poppett' once lived there, has disappeared. I suppose the people who look after Campden did not consider it necessary to keep these damp and insanitary but picturesque relics of the past.

Campden always considered itself more genteel than the other villages around and in the early nineteenth century had a rhymster who enjoyed making up rude doggerel about its more rustic neighbours, particularly those at Ebrington, a couple of miles away. This pride may have been an inheritance from the days when Campden was a town of the Staple, when king's officers and important merchants were frequent visitors, settling dues for the wool bought and sold, and who probably brought London ways with them that the Campden people would have liked to emulate.

That was Campden's golden age, when wealthy wool-men could

Sir Robert Dover on Dover's Hill

build themselves substantial houses from the good white Guiting stone from the town's quarries at Westington and who had the means to erect a handsome church to help their souls to heaven. The quarry is still there and has provided stone for many buildings since those days, moving away from the original site as it became worked out and leaving it a series of hollows and humps overgrown with trees. I think one could work out the periods of the various rebuildings and renovating of the town by the different hollows left by succeeding generations of quarrymen and the age of the vegetation grown over the old workings, including a stone-mine now closed because it became unsafe to work, or because the new safety regulations about the shoring up of mines proved too expensive.

View of Chipping Campden and Meon Hill from the conduit on Westington Hill

Wandering about this wilderness, I once found a long-tailed tit's nest hanging from a blackthorn bush, and as the fledglings had flown I took it down and soon grew tired of counting the hundreds of feathers making up the bottle-shaped nest held together by fine grass stems. Another form of building and much warmer, I told myself, than some of those old cold, damp, stone cottages that sheltered the people of Campden when the quarry first provided the stone for their walls.

The last big benefactor of Campden was the late F. L. Griggs RA, who, when Dover's Hill (the town's splendid breathing place where Dover once held his games) was put up for sale as a suitable site for a hotel, bought it to gain time to organize support and rouse public

73

opinion, lest it be lost to the town. Griggs wanted it to be an open space for ever, but he was not a wealthy man and took the risk. The appeal brought in over £2,000, but £4,000 was needed. The balance was given by Professor C. M. Trevelyan, another lover of Campden, and Dover's Hill was conveyed to the National Trust in December 1928. Another good deed Griggs did was to use his influence to get the Electricity Board to put the wires and poles in the High Street underground or behind the town so that the famous street should not be spoilt by a network of them. Campden has always been fortunate in its friends.

Campden's most characteristic buildings are scheduled under the Town and Country Planning Act 1957 Section 40, but no Act or Trust can preserve a place if the inhabitants are indifferent to its welfare. Newcomers to Campden, the retired who have bought the old cottages and houses, are for the most part aware of its unique quality. It was in most cases the reason they came to live in Campden.

Though in the same parish, Broad Campden is no mere appendage of Chipping Campden but a village in its own right with a church, a Quaker meeting house, a pub that is a true 'local' and, lining its long, wide street, houses and cottages roofed in a cosy thatch of splendid quality. The dwellings have pretty gardens, well-trimmed hedges, plentiful garden trees, their modern additions never intruding on the rural scene. It is as picturesque a village as any in the south-west and though in the heart of Cotswold country does not entirely belong to it.

Amid the charming if rather fussy trimmings, one building stands out, elegantly simple in design, built of good ashlar with a stone-tiled roof, mullioned windows and a plain rounded hood-mould over the doorway. It was built in 1663 and enlarged in 1667. Behind it was a burial ground where many prominent Quakers were buried, including Jonathan Hull, who invented an early version of the steamboat. (It is interesting that weavers, tanners, dyers and other craftsmen made up the bulk of the members, obviously men of independent ideas who were not dominated by the landowners whose word was law in rural districts at that time.) It is probable that George Fox rode over from Armscote in Warwickshire where there was another early meeting house, to encourage his brothers, for the period between Cromwell's death and the Restoration was one

Quakers' Meeting House, Broad Campden

of dire trouble for the Quakers. In 1660 Edward Warner, Thomas Moseley, Thomas Keite and others were brought before Sir Thomas Overbury of Bourton-on-the-Hill charged with holding a meeting at Broad Campden; although sympathetic towards freedom of thought, Overbury was obliged to commit them to the county gaol. The meeting house fell into decay in the 1880s, having been used for other purposes, but in 1960 it was restored, and now it functions again.

I like to go to Weston Subedge by the steep road west of Dover's Hill, a hollow way overshadowed by trees that seem taller then they are because of the high banks on which they grow. The road after winding and turning comes out into a rambling village, a mixture of stone and half-timbered cottages set among orchards and large gardens. The most distinguished-looking house, in the Elizabethan style of gables, finials and tall, diagonally set chimneys, is said to have associations with Bishop Latimer.

An old Field Account book for Weston Subedge, one of the last villages to be enclosed on Cotswold, printed by C. R. Ashbee, gives fascinating details of how the parishioners used to plant their common fields. At a meeting at the vestry in 1849 they decided to 'plant a field called Gravels with vetches, another with beans, another with wheat, and sheep were not to be allowed to feed on the young wheat until after Christmas next', an entry I find rather puzzling. Each year the parishioners swore to weed properly, hoe, manure and cultivate the fields. Entries include the cost of labour, as when it is put down that for fifteen days keeping birds off the beans and wheat the payment was five shillings. Presumably the bird-scarer was a child. It seems a pitiful return for fifteen long and lonely days in the field chasing those devilishly ingenious birds rooks, crows and magpies.

In *Footpath Ways in Gloucestershire*, Algernon Gissing tells how his old friend the parish clerk would discuss the last hayward of the open field system, who, when it came to an end, found himself a job as an 'errands man for a grocer in Campden'. The name of the last hayward was Giles Cockbill, and I see him in my mind's eye as a stout, red-faced man with a billycock hat bleached by sun and rain, buttoned gaiters and a tough linen smock, and even when he lost his official position still keeping an air of self-importance.

Aston Subedge has the same kinship with both vale and hills as its larger neighbour, the same kind of rambling gardens and orchard that in the spring are loud with the songs of chaffinches, and it also has its typical old manor-house in the Cotswold style, three tall gabled dormers with ball finials, mullioned and transomed windows and a continuous drip-mould over the windows of the ground floor. It is said Prince Rupert stayed here for the first Dover's Games. Endymion Porter, who was born here in 1587 and who became an ambassador of Charles I, supplied Robert Dover with a suit of fine yellow clothes and a befeathered hat, cast-offs of the King, so he could make a dashing appearance at the Games.

In spring both Weston and Aston Subedge are ablow with plum and apple blossom, part of the show put on by the Vale of Evesham orchards which local people look forward to visiting in excursions along the flowery lanes of the Vale between the orchards in full bloom. I remember on one occasion driving along the lanes with the wind sending showers of plum and pear-blossom petals whirling down to cover the car and the road with fallen petals so I seemed to be driving through a scented snowstorm.

Willersey is another of those villages that spread from the hill into the Vale, and the difference between these villages that have their feet in the Vale and their heads in the hills is that they have more room to spread themselves, not being confined to a narrow fold in the hills like true hill villages – Blockley, for example, Bourton-on-the-Hill, Ebrington and Buckland.

Willersey has a village green and a duckpond, amenities more usually found in neighbouring Warwickshire, and its houses are ranged on either side of the green, giving the village a splendid focal point. Pool House, said by David Verey to be late seventeenth century, looks as if it has not always fared well during its long life; its gateposts seem a little too imposing as the house appears today, but with the pond and its ducks as foreground it makes a pretty rural picture. Another interesting house, as showing what can happen to old houses on Cotswold, is one originally a farmhouse but which was moved a quarter of a mile up the hill and rebuilt much larger by A. N. Prentice in 1912.

Saintbury once had many more houses and a mill on the lower road but they have disappeared, and now it is almost entirely a small upland village with its houses tucked away in haphazard fashion as if wishing to hide from the world below. Its church of St Nicholas, despite its miniature size, contains a memorial of every phase of its life, from Saxon to the Arts and Crafts Revival of the 1900s. It also has the remains of a yew tree that could be as old as the original church. It was still growing in 1936, though much decayed.

Ryknild Street or Buckle Street, Weston Subedge

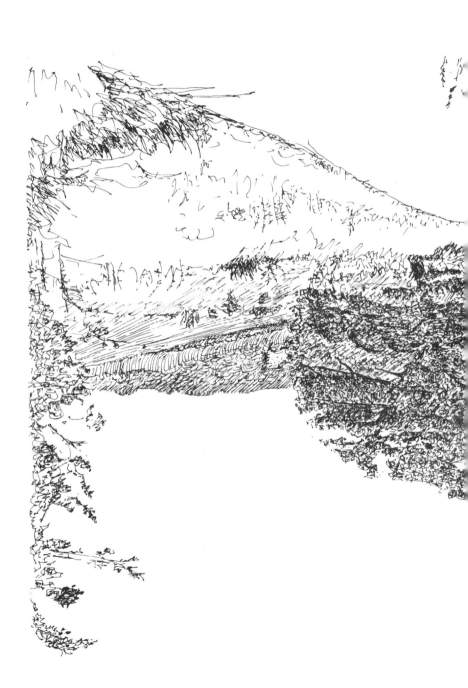

Pool House, Willersey

St Nicholas's isolated setting under the edge makes it possible for it to be seen from all sides, and from the Vale its spire, gleaming white as ivory against its green background, makes a good landmark for the wayfarer. Its offerings from the past are a battered stone figure set in the jamb of the windows of the chancel, supposed to be of the eleventh century, two early Norman doorways, one having a tympanum of diaper patterning, and jambs with zigzags and voluted capitals. The rest of the church is mainly thirteenth and fourteenth century, including the tower and broach-spire. Its latest addition is a simple candle chandelier of wrought iron from C. R. Ashbee, given in 1911 to celebrate the birth of a daughter. Whether it is the open situation or because one comes to it as a climax to a pretty embowered village or for some reason I cannot fathom, I always think of it as a happy church, without the gloom and mouldy smell of outworn faith and outworn grief one so often associates with remote ancient churches. Perhaps something of the sunny temper of its old parish clerk about whom Algernon Gissing wrote so affectionately still hangs about it.

8 · Stow-on-the-Wold and Broadwell

Stow-on-the-Wold – where, as the old rhyme says and any inhabitant will tell you, 'the wind blows cold', or in another version, 'the Devil caught cold' – is one of the few Cotswold villages to be set on a hilltop. The original settlement was at Maugersbury, just below the exposed top of the hill, where there are traces of an Iron Age camp and where coins of Bodvic, the Belgic chief of the Dobunni whose headquarters were at Bagendon, have been found.

Stow owes it creation to the Foss Way which, after climbing three hundred feet in a mile, comes to a junction at the hilltop with the ancient Cotswold Ridgeway, thus, in the old days, ensuring a meeting place for travellers from all directions. It is still such a meeting place today. The monks of Evesham Abbey, who owned Maugersbury, saw this junction as the ideal spot for a market that would bring them considerable profit in tolls, and they issued a charter decreeing that Stow, or Edwardstow as it was then called, should become a port or unfortified marketplace. By the late fifteenth century two annual fairs as well as the weekly market were well established, and since then, and indeed before, Stow has been a local shopping centre and a place of call for travellers. Its brief interlude as an industrial town making boots and shoes has been forgotten, though there used to be an absurd reminder in the pair of stone boots used as plinths to the fluted pilasters of St Edward's House, an eighteenth-century building whose once elegant façade has come down in the world. The stone boots were there in the 1920s but have now been replaced by what looks like the original plinths. I always regarded them as an instance of a Cotsaller's use of stone in preference to any other material, even to advertise his boot factory.

In our great-grandparents' days, Stow Fair was the place where villagers could reckon on meeting old friends and relatives from villages around, for it was as important a date in their calendars as

Stow-on-the-Wold

Christmas or the Whitsuntide Club Outing. It was also a day that was used as a reckoning rod, for when I asked one old lady how old she was, she told me she would be eighty next Stow Fair, and another told me she would have been married fifty years come Stow Fair. Francis Witt, rector of Upper Slaughter from 1808 to 1854, wrote in his diary for 22 October 1829 that he had left Gloucester earlier than he wished because the tradespeople expected their bills to be paid at Stow Fair, where creditors and debtors met.

If a farmer had a horse for sale at the fair, the carter would have to start very early in the morning after grooming the horse, polishing its hoofs and plaiting coloured ribbons into mane and tail so it would look its best when paraded up and down the road in front of prospective buyers. If he made a reasonable sale, the farmer would treat him to a drink at the Unicorn, a good sale and there might be a little tip slipped into his hand, but if he did not sell the horse he

83

would have to walk all the way back to the farm with it. My old carter friend told me of such an experience with a rueful twinkle, age having made him see humour in such incidents.

'It rained and the wind blew so you couldn't see where you were going, and the rain poured off that poor horse's flanks like a waterspout. He was a big horse and I kept in the burra of his belly and got a bit of shelter. I gave him a good rub down and an extra handful of corn, the boss not being around, and the wife had saved me a basin of stew and had a good fire going so I was soon warm and dry. Farmer was a bit sheepish-like next morning the way he'd served me not even a drop of cider for all my trouble. He was sneezing something awful, grumbling he'd caught cold sitting in the open trap, so I reckon I had the best of it after all, walking and the old horse keeping me warm.'

The buying and selling of horses and ponies now goes on in a field, not in the street as before, which is easier for through traffic but it has taken some of the colour and excitement from the fair. However, the amusement fair still comes, with its roundabouts and sideshows, and if one cannot come away with a china dog or a Staffordshire figure as a fairing, one can win a tiny goldfish in a plastic bag.

A glimpse of the pleasures of the local gentry in the early nineteenth century comes in an entry of Francis Witt's diary for December 1828, where he notes the poor church attendance of the trustees of the Stow Provident Bank because of the ball at the Unicorn Inn the night before, after a meeting of the Hunt when the Duke of Beaufort's hounds drew off at Adlestrop Gate. The ball took place in a 'new and handsome room erected by subscription', under the presidency of Lord Edward Somerset. A grimmer view of life at that time is provided by the story of the murder of E. J. Rens, actuary of the Stow Provident Bank, who was murdered near the horse-pool at Stow by three men who robbed him of his gold watch and purse. 'For many months,' wrote Francis Witt, 'the roads have swarmed with sturdy and ferocious-looking vagabonds.'

Francis Witt was related to the Tracey family of Stanway through his grandmother, dined at all the best houses in the district and was frank in his diary about his neighbours and any other important people who came his way. Writing of the Duke of Gloucester making his annual visit to the new spa of Cheltenham, he described him as aged in appearance, vacant in countenance, 'but retains a princely air with a strong family resemblance to his Royal Race'. And with a certain amount of relish, I feel, Witt puts down his son's opinion of Lord John Russell, then canvassing as prospective candidate for Stroud, as 'a mean-looking bilious person'.

Witt had little sympathy for the poor and no sentimentality about wrongdoers. Obliged to suspend the examination of a prisoner for a few hours, he sent him back to the lock-up meanwhile, and when an officer was sent to fetch the prisoner, he was found dead, having strangled himself. The charge against the man was stealing from a blind man's box. 'A wretched example of living without God in the world, a wild reckless hardened life of idleness and vice,' Witt wrote.

In happier mood he tells of the Coronation Day of Queen Victoria, fortunately a fine day in Stow for the dinner for four hundred in the market-place, with beef, mutton and beer. On returning home to Upper Slaughter, Francis Witt and his wife distributed cake, cheese and beer to forty children of the Sunday School. It is surprising to learn that as late as 1838 children were given beer to drink, but it was probably the smallest of small beer and safer to drink than their water-supply.

Taking the old road to Broadwell at the west end of Stow down the steep hill to the Evenlode valley, one passes a watering-place on a narrow platform on the hillside surrounded by a low stone wall. It used to be called a Roman well in my young days, but that was when the name Roman was applied to any piece of medieval carved or worked stone re-used in another building, before we all became knowledgeable about antiquities through looking at television.

Broadwell today seems enclosed in woodland, as if Wychford Forest once upon a time not so very far away had renewed itself about the village. It is as glossy and gentrified as any secluded Cotswold village taken over by the wealthy and retired. It has also the Alpine Nurseries of Joe Elliot in an old barn to bring visitors who wander around the beds of miniature mountain plants translated into a Cotswold valley, both visitors and plants looking quite happy to be there.

Broadwell churchyard has a good collection of table tombs, including some with 'bale' tops dating from 1601–12. Could there have been a local mason who learned his trade from the Burford masons who originated this kind of tomb? There is also another large table tomb of early date with the simplest of ornament carved on its heavy stones, and eight kneeling 'weepers' all alike, four on each side and strangely appealing in their ritual expression of grief.

The village of Lower Swell is in the Dikler valley a mile west of Stow, the little river with its yellow mimulus and stands of pink

Stow well

willowherb part of the village scene. The cottages have an appearance of quiet domesticity contrasting with the prehistory of the higher ground surrounding it, for on the old Cow Common are neolithic long barrows and Bronze Age tumuli, and running across it Condicote Lane, a prehistoric trackway which the Romans straightened so that it became called 'Street' in the Saxon charters of that area.

David Royce, rector of Lower Swell and archaeologist, picked up most of the worked flints in his collection locally, and the little Norman church where he preached was erected on a tumulus, the builders using the tump to raise the church higher. A prehistoric cremation was found in the churchyard, and the Saxon left their mark by giving Swell its name and incising two dials on the church walls, while nearby the Romans had a burial ground. There is a tympanum over the Norman doorway showing the Tree of Life, with a fat dove sitting on one of the spreading branches, said by experts to be of pagan origin. I think it suits the little church perfectly as a symbol of the continuity of life in the neighbourhood from prehistoric times onward.

The eighteenth century also left its memorial, but this is beyond the village on the road leading to Stow, where there is a façade on a cottage over a chalybeate spring, all that remains of an attempt to turn Lower Swell into a spa at a time when spas were becoming fashionable. But fortunately, or unfortunately according to the way you look at it, the vicinity did not have the attractions of Cheltenham or Leamington to offer visitors – no assembly room, no promenade, no shops. The façade looks forlorn today, a forgotten footnote to a project to benefit from nature's healing waters.

Upper Swell lies a mile north of Lower, and the way to it is from Stow on the road that dips and rises with a lilting rhythm as it drops three hundred feet to the mill on the Dikler at the beginning of the village. When we walked from Stow, we went quietly to look over the walls lest we disturbed a kingfisher who haunted that stretch of the water, but there were always dragonflies, the large ones with big heads and menacing eyes and the pretty blue demoiselles.

South of the mill the Dikler flows through Abbotswood, whose water-gardens are famous in the neighbourhood, and then the village comes into view. Both the Swells and the Slaughters have a large percentage of retired people who have modernized the old cottages, filling the gardens with roses and flowering shrubs that riot luxuriantly in the summer, almost obliterating the cottage walls, making a pastoral haven of country life modern style. Without the newcomers many of these little old cottages would have mouldered away into ruins and been lost.

Upper Slaughter is on the Eye brook, a tributary of the Dikler. It was the home of the Reverend Francis Witt, the diarist, rector of the parish and lord of the manor, who died in 1854. There is a mortuary chapel north of the chancel built to house his tomb, which has a memorial brass and is set in a recess decorated fourteenth-century fashion. The Old Manor House, mainly an Elizabethan building with gables, has a Jacobean porch of two storeys with Doric pilasters below and Ionic above, with a frieze and semi-circular pediment. The home of the Witt family, now a hotel, was the old parsonage.

Lower Slaughter has become one of Cotswold's tourist attractions, with the river, with its charming little bridges and grassy banks, and an old mill built of brick completing the picture like an illustration

Tomb with carved weepers, Broadwell

to a Victorian ballad and giving an old-world aspect to the village.
The manor-house was built by Valentine Strong, one of the family of
master masons from Taynton and Barrington. Being forward-looking
and associated with London's rebuilding after the Great Fire, he did
not give this house the Tudor look but chose a square, plain structure,
the excellent proportions of doors and windows giving the manor-
house the necessary dignity. In one of the basement rooms there
used to be a mural inscription, an address to the servants: 'A good
character is valuable to everyone but specially to servants for it is
their bread and without it they cannot be admitted into a creditable
family, and happy it is that the best of characters is in everyone's
power to deserve. RICHARD WHITE 1771. The Whitmore family lived
in the house from the seventeenth century until 1964, when the estate
was sold, so perhaps Richard White was its major-domo, another
Malvolio to the servants in his charge.

Bourton-on-the-Water, a popular resort, is on the site of a Roman
settlement. It has many extras much appreciated by tourists, but

Donnington Brewery and lake, Dikler valley

they have nothing to do with Cotswold. There are many things to amuse children as well as adults: Birdland, the model village with its miniature replica of the village, gift- and tea-shops and in the summer an unending supply of ice-cream and lollies. Its position on the Foss makes it easily accessible, and it is a favourite calling place for coaches, adequate parking space making this possible, and Bourton having wide streets with room for people as well as cars. The most delightful part is its little river, with picturesque bridges, willow trees and wide grass verges where one can stroll and enjoy the scene. Bourton has a leisurely air about it, and the winds do not blow as cold there as in many other Cotswold villages. There are some handsome stone houses old and new and a Georgian church built by William Marshall, the eighteenth-century Gloucestershire agriculturist, the authority on farming in his day, who lived at Bourton long before it became a tourist centre.

Bourton Bridge on the Foss is on the site of a Roman bridge over the river replacing a ford in the sixth century, a stone bridge in 1483 a country bridge in 1806, and it was rebuilt again in 1959.

Bourton has seen many centuries come and go. There was once an Iron-Age settlement at Salmonsbury camp near the town, then a Roman settlement, and it found favour with the Saxons, as one would expect because of its good water-supply, fertile soil and woodland, for they had a considerable homestead between the Foss and today's village. Remains of a Saxon upright loom with loom weights and pottery were found there, now in the British Museum.

Today Bourton is a residential area for commuters from the Midlands, Stow and Cirencester, a flourishing little town which has its own life when the visitors depart and it settles into its winter calm.

Jacobean porch, Upper Swell manor

9 · Cirencester and the Churn Valley

The most distant source of the many tributaries making up the Thames is Seven Springs near Coberley, where the River Churn is born of many springs issuing from an ornamental hollow with a plume of beeches above. It then flows south-easterly across Cotswold through four big estates, Coberley, Cowley, Colesbourne and Rendcomb, and in the days when wealthy landowners attempted to outrival one another in landscaping their pleasure grounds, the river became a plaything all the way from Seven Springs to Cirencester.

Coberley's great mansion has been lost for nearly two hundred years. A wall at the east end of the churchyard with Renaissance openings on the far side is all that remains of it, but the church still stands. The estate first belonged to the Berkeleys, then the Brydges, Chandos and Castlemain families in that order – names that occur again and again in national as well as local history. A reminder of the Berkeleys is the chapel built as a chantry in 1340, having a window so placed that the sanctus bell could be heard from the house. It also has an ancient tenor bell inscribed '*AVE MARIA GRACIA PLENA*' with the 'Royal Heads Stamps' of Edward III and Queen Philippa as word stops.

The church is rich in Berkeley memorials, one a 'heart' burial, in the form of a small bust of a knight in chain mail, Sir Giles de Berkeley, holding a heart in his hands over a shield at his breast. A low mound on the ground outside the chancel is said to cover the remains of Lombard, Sir Giles's horse, and for an animal to be buried openly in consecrated ground in the thirteenth century gives one an idea of the power of the Berkeley family in those days. It is to be hoped that no inquisitive digger-up of ancient tumps will excavate the mound, for there is little purpose in spoiling a good legend for a problematical truth.

By the time the Churn reaches the tree-shaded, bird-haunted lake of Cowley, it has become fully grown, and by the time it has left its artificially widened waters behind it has gathered enough force to serve a couple of mills. None of them functions now but it is interesting that Trinity Mill, in working order in 1970, has a doorway leading directly from the main bedroom of the millhouse to the mill so that the miller could see if the wheel was functioning properly when he was in bed. One of the medieval mills on the Coln had a similar arrangement, for in a narrow building attached to the mill was the abode of the miller's man, with a tiny bedchamber with a squint through the wall so he could see the wheel from his narrow bed. A small niche in the wall provided a safe place for his candlestick and, one hopes, a bottle of something warming as well if he had to get up in the night and attend to the wheel.

The main road once left the Churn valley to cross the river at Cockleford, but in 1825 a new road was developed to avoid the river-crossing and the sharp pull up Bubb's Hill to High Cross, notorious in the old days for accidents to coaches and waggons. Many a High-Flyer carrying His Majesty's mails in the old days came to grief there in bad weather. In a little over a mile the old road comes to Elkstone, a bleak village that lies in a no-man's-land between two main roads both leading to Cirencester. It looks swept bare by the chill winds that haunt the place all the year round, with the splendid church standing in gaunt Norman pride to startle visitors by the ferocity of its carvings of scowling dragons and rows of sharp teeth snarling to scare the ungodly into hell.

The carving is still crisp, the stone being an excellent freestone that weathers well, and after all these years (the church is dated 1160) one can still feel the vitality of the mason-carver who wielded his adze unerringly. The entrance arch has carvings of men and animals guarding the way in and warning any who would enter with evil intent. On the tower, built two hundred years later there are four gargoyles whose large heads contrast unpleasantly with the emaciated arms holding up the thick, ugly body. Less threatening figures playing medieval instruments are carved on the buttresses, and we see that two hundred years after the building of the original church the Cotswold stone-carvers had not lost their skill, though now they used a chisel more often than an adze. One of the gentler pieces of decoration is the boss of the vault over the chancel which has the carving of a bead-studded buckle looking as if it had drawn the ribs together and secured them safely. The only other instance of this device is at Kilpeck in Herefordshire.

Elkstone's church is a complete contrast to the little church at Syde, which huddles down on a narrow shelf on the hillside so close to barns and other farm buildings that it seems part of the farm complex. In the lane coming up to Syde is a cottage with fourteenth-century windows which could have belonged to a chantry chapel founded by a steward of the Berkeley family; he wrote of one of his duties: 'Att Syde to fynde a pryste to celebrate and pray for the said founders . . . to live chastely and nott come to marketts alehouses or Tavernes neither shall he frequent unlawful Games.' At the west end of one of the buildings about the church are two small traceried windows which are thought to have belonged to a priest's lodging, so William the Steward could have found his chantry priest to pray for his soul.

The new road follows the river valley, taking the rise more gently and meandering through water-meadows that used to be 'drowned' in the old days to give an earlier bite for the cattle. It needed an experienced 'drowner' to attend to the sluices or the results could be disastrous. This is one of the crafts being lost now they are no longer needed, but I remember seeing in a Wiltshire valley not so long ago meadows newly 'drowned' and admiring the vivid emerald green of the grass lighting up the valley landscape.

On its way the road is bordered by the woods and plantations of Cowley and Colesbourne and the steep-wooded slopes of Rendcomb, where I hope the badgers still find a safe haven. It is one of the pleasantest main roads crossing Cotswold, for it follows the contours of the hills, curving in gentle gradients with prospects on both sides pleasing to the kind of traveller whose aim is not only to reach a destination but to enjoy the journey.

Colesbourne Park has a living memorial to a great naturalist, H. J. Elmes, who lived there and between 1906 and 1913 wrote his seven-volume classic work on British trees. He planted many exotic trees on the estate, the result of his travels round the world looking for trees, butterflies and game birds. He was also a breeder of Cotswold sheep.

Sir Edmund Tame owned the manor of Rendcomb. He was the son of John Tame, the wool-man who was building the great church at Fairford when he died; Sir Edmund completed it and then went on to rebuild Rendcomb, a complete rebuilding in the Perpendicular style though late for the period. It has many interesting features including a lock plate on the south door with the Arabic numerals 1527, which does not suggest a local blacksmith unless he worked to a design given him by Sir Edmund, who travelled far on his business affairs. The Norman font is of a kind rarely seen on Cotswold and is said to have been brought by the Guise family from Elmore. Around it is an arcade with cylindrical shafts containing eleven figures of the apostles, the twelfth being left empty to signify Judas, and around the top of the bowl a fret-band pattern linking it with the font in Hereford Cathedral. Rendcomb is now a boys' school, the church used by the boys as a chapel, and it is very beautifully kept.

Sir F. H. Goldsmidt, who bought the new estate in 1863, built two bridges made necessary after the construction of a new drive to Rendcomb House. The bridge over the village road is of iron with ornamental balustrading supported on high stone pillars; the river bridge is more decorative, having three arches and a keystone with a mask of a river god and stone balustrades.

The Churn comes out of the Rendcomb woods into the open at North Cerney, a village with some good stone houses, cottages with large windows which presumably were occupied by weavers in the past, for they needed more light than the ordinary cottage windows provided, and a church containing so many curious and beautiful things that it is like a special museum. The benefactor was William Iveson Croome, who devoted half a century or more to beautifying the church. Two Gothic figures of the fifteenth century, a Virgin of French origin and two bishops from south Germany on the reredos were given by him to replace statues smashed or removed during the Reformation. William Whitchurch, once Abbot of Winchcombe Abbey, was uncle to the Rector who rebuilt the nave after a fire in 1470, and the north window is a memorial to him, gift of John Eycote, curate, whose figure appears under the crucifix.

The oldest house in the village is the Old Church House on the south side of the churchyard; the combination of rectory, church and the Old Church House makes an attractive grouping, so one sees again how on Cotswold the older buildings stand on the best sites to enhance their grace and dignity.

With Cirencester only two miles away, the Churn in its valley passes Baunton, a village perched high on the hills on the White Way. (For those who prefer the hills an exhilarating way to reach Cirencester is to follow the White Way and then come down into the town past Car Barrows and the Spital Gate.) For many years Baunton resisted the pull of Cirencester, keeping a close kinship with the hills, so that its large painting of St Christopher, the patron saint of

travellers, seemed to have a special meaning. But that splendid complex of Manor Farm of barns, a great tithe barn, granaries, talluts, cart porches on pillars and the seventeenth-century farmhouse, when I last saw it in 1984, was being altered and reorganized and there seemed to be more building going on in the village. Baunton's proximity to Cirencester makes it very vulnerable, especially today, when so many people want to live on Cotswold even if it means commuting daily; in moments of depression one wonders if Cotswold villages will finally develop into a new kind of suburbia, until one reminds oneself that change is inevitable and preferable to death. But I hope the Manor Farm will survive entire; it is such a splendid example of the more spacious days of the late eighteenth century when farm buildings as well as the manor-house were designed as a dignified whole, showing the wealth and good taste of the landowner and, in the case of Baunton's Manor Farm, a secure and comfortable homestead in the hills, with animals, buildings and farming folk enclosed in a great courtyard which, when the great doors of the archway leading into it were closed, became a fastness against the worst of the weather and hostile marauders, as in medieval times.

Leaving North Cerney, the river and the main road make their way south, passing first a minor way to Bagendon and then south in another mile for the road but a more generous mile and a half of meandering river to come to Cirencester. Taking the road to Bagendon, one is at once in a different kind of country, secretive, secluded. Bagendon must be one of the most exciting names for the historian and prehistorian of Cotswold. Coming to it there was little to see of its pre-Roman existence in the days when the earthworks about the village puzzled antiquaries and archaeologists; then Mrs Elsie Clifford's inspiration and excavation proved it to be the site of the capital of the eastern Dobunni before the conquering Romans moved them to a new capital, Cirencester. Now in the Corinium Museum in Cirencester are some of the many treasures she found, proving without doubt that the natives the Romans found when they invaded Britain were not the woad-painted savages of the old history books but a people with as many if not more artistic and practical skills then the Romans themselves and the same taste for good living; long before the Romans came, they imported wine, oil, pottery, glass from Syria and other luxuries, in return sending wool, hides, coarse cloth,

Rendcomb, Norman font

slaves and hunting dogs. Mrs Clifford's book, *A Belgic Oppidum*, gives a detailed and fascinating history of her findings.

The people living at Bagendon had buildings with stone foundations, walls of wattle and daub, roofs of thatch, probably similar to the dwellings occupied by farmworkers in the Middle Ages and until the eighteenth century and even later, when landowners beautifying their estates built cottages for their workers that would not disgrace the rest of the estate. The eastern Dobunni were farmers and kept large herds of cattle and flocks of sheep. Immense quantities of bones of oxen were found, linking up with the export of hides, and the sheep provided the wool for weaving the coarse cloth or cloaks we know were exported, for they are in the list of exports kept by Strabo in 10 BC. The metalwork found was of high quality, and there is a brooch of a pattern particular to Bagendon smiths.

The trackways that come very near to Bagendon and those that go on to cross the Severn must have been very busy in the half century or so when the Dobunni under Bodvic occupied it, bringing gold from Wales, iron from the forest of Dean and lead from the Mendips. They seem to have used coal as well as charcoal in their furnaces. They minted their own coins, the gold ones having their emblem, a tree device, impressed on them, while the reverse was the triple-tailed horse used by other Belgic tribes.

There is no evidence on the site that the take-over by the Romans was resisted, unlike the evidence of massacre at Bredon and elsewhere when an incursion of Belgic people swept northwards through Wessex and then established their capital at Bagendon. Now they in their turn were evicted but it was a bloodless eviction, and as the Dobunni were accustomed to the luxuries of Roman civilization long before the invasion, they must have accepted Romanization willingly. The leaders and chiefs seem to have done so while the ordinary people went on working at their various trades and occupations in the way they had always done.

By the time the Anglo-Saxons had settled in the valley of the Churn, nature had covered the old capital of the Dobunni with scrub and rough woodland, and by the time the little Norman church had been altered to become a chapel of the Weavers' Guild of Cirencester in the fifteenth century, not even a tradition remained that Bagendon had once been a flourishing city. The general explanation of the lengths of bank and ditch about the village was that they had been thrown up in 536 by the Britons in defence against Cedric, King of the West Saxons.

Weavers' Hall, Thomas Street, Cirencester

The Trinity Chapel in Cirencester church belonged to the Weavers' Guild at that time, and a chamber in the tower of Bagendon church provided lodgings for the priests sent from Cirencester on holy days to take the services. Fragments of medieval Glass in the south window of the chancel include a St Catherine's Wheel and a Latin reference to the 'priests of the Chantry of the Holy Trinity'.

Corinium, or Cirencester, began as a town the Romans made for the Dobunni to replace their capital at Bagendon. It was easier for the provincial administrators of Rome to keep an eye on them on the plain and gather their tributes of corn, hides, wool and coarse cloth and export these commodities from a place where three through-roads met, the Foss, Akeman Street and Ermine Street. From about AD 70 and for well over 150 years the Dobunni suffered no serious infiltration from the Saxons, but by the end of the fourth century the Saxons had made serious inroads into Cotswold, the natives having little power to resist once the Romans had withdrawn their armies.

The modern documented history of Cirencester begins with the abbey founded by Henry I, though evidence that a Saxon church once stood on the site was discovered when the abbey ruins were excavated. But it was the wool industry providing the wealth for the abbey which culminated in the rebuilding of the abbey church in 1530. The abbot with his market tolls, his great gathering of wool from the sheep-walks of his many manors, had generated considerable riches for his abbey but did not bring much benefit to the town, and at the Dissolution the church survived as the parish church, catering for the people of the town as well as for the nobles and important churchmen. Within its shelter the craftsmen's guilds had their own chapels and halls, and it must have been a splendid place at the height of its glory before the Reformation, when its chantry chapels were furnished by rich wool-men. The Trinity Chapel belonged to the Weavers' Guild, as we know by the will of a member of the Guild, which also built the Weavers' Hall in Thomas Street, the oldest secular building in the town. Outwardly it is austere, almost forbidding, its stone weathered to an antique grey with small rectangular windows and a four-centred arch doorway with a defaced image above, probably St Thomas or the founder, Sir William Nottingham, who died in 1437.

The town has so many buildings of architectural interest in the old streets around the Market Square that it can take many days to discover all the treasures. Dollar Street, Thomas Street, Coxwell Street, Gloucester Street and many others offer a collection of seventeenth- and eighteenth-century buildings surviving with little alteration externally. In the tourist season it is better to take one's perambulations in the evening or early morning because of the heavy traffic on the roads and busy shoppers on the pavements with little patience for loiterers. I once spent a week of evenings in this way, walking for a couple of hours or so after an evening meal, each evening a voyage of discovery.

Cirencester is another Cotswold town that has served travellers from the days when the Roman roads were the main highways, and there are many inns not only in the town itself but on the roads approaching it. Akeman Street, once so busy, however, is now no more than a lane with the remains of turnpike milestones on the route to Ready Token, an inn where, it is said, cash and not credit was the rule. These points of call along a highroad had many ways of knowing when a coach was to be expected, apart from those with regular timetables, which could be upset by bad weather and accidents such as a wheel coming off, a common occurrence on a bad stretch of road. According to an account in the *Wilts and Glos Standard* of 1851, a look-out was erected on the roof of the house, and when a lumbering coach was seen in the distance, 'the joint was put on the spit, the condiments in the pot' and a meal made ready for the travellers when they arrived. This road along part of the valley of the Churn was the recognized route to Fairford and London.

With the end of the wool and then the clothing trade Cirencester declined, but not as badly as Northleach and Chipping Campden, for it had a big house to take the place of the abbey and guide its affairs from the middle of the eighteenth century at least. The first Earl of Bathurst, of Cirencester Park, was a man of tremendous vitality, a friend and patron of the eighteenth-century poets and satirists Pope, Gay and Swift, and many were the anecdotes they told about him. He became obsessed with the idea of improving his estate, levelling out hills and altering water courses, and in these projects Alexander Pope was his encourager. The two men revelled in the job, feeling no doubt a godlike power in removing mountains, albeit little ones, and changing the flow of the waters of the earth. It must have been a heady business, especially as they had labour enough and were wealthy enough to enjoy it. Pope wrote an incredible number of couplets about these changes, urbane, fulsome and many of them dull.

The world of politics and letters to which Lord Bathurst belonged by birth and earlier inclination began to take second place as the wide acres of Cirencester Park became his playground and as his ideas became more eccentric – such as adding artificial ruins to his avenues and green vistas to give them a romantic aura, while Pope had his own little 'bower' as he called it, known now as 'Pope's Seat', a vermiculated, rusticated stone pavilion. Burke wrote of Lord Bathurst's many virtues 'which have made him one of the most amiable as he was one of the most fortunate men of his day', and making allowances for the way poets at that period were expected to extol their patrons, Lord Bathurst does seem to have been a man of extraordinary talents. We should be thankful today that he planted many thousands of trees that those coming after him could enjoy, one of the finest examples in England of planting in the pre-landscape manner. Looking at the buildings and the splendid avenues of trees, one feels that his heart was more in horticulture than in building.

Though not in the valley of the Churn, Sapperton comes into the domain of Cirencester Park. It lies some five miles west of the town if one walks through the park from the entrance of Cicely Street, first along the wide path to the ruins of Alfred's House in Oakley Wood and then on to the junction of the ten rides spread out fanwise into Sapperton Wood. From there one soon arrives at the village along the road that is on the line of one of Cotswold's ancient trackways leading out of Cotswold into Wiltshire.

Sapperton has its own historian in Norman Jewson, though it was not his intention originally to produce a local history when he wrote *By Chance I Did Rove* in 1920, reprinted in 1973. His purpose was, as he explained, to put down his recollections of Sapperton from the time when he first went to live there as a young man, to describe the district which he explored by walking, to tell stories of the old craftsmen who lived there and to describe the life and work of Ernest Gimson, the Barnsley brothers and their fellow craftsmen whose company he joined in 1907. Originally trained as an architect in London, when he came to Sapperton to work under Gimson he acquired a working knowledge of the subsidiary crafts, furniture-making, metalwork, plasterwork, designs for embroidery and carving, indeed any form of craft that gave a fuller understanding of man's need to improve his home and environment. I remember particularly his showing me a child's small chair which he had made, which he regarded as a kind of doodle. It was round-backed, small enough to fit a toddler's back comfortably, the struts holding the back being characters from children's classics, each most lovingly executed and coloured. I could imagine a child's exploring fingers deriving a certain reassurance from the figures in the same way as a favourite toy can bring comfort.

When I first met Norman Jewson, he was in his eighties, tall, thin, still gallant and a splendid story-teller. One of his regrets was that he was no longer allowed to climb the tall ladder to trim the spectacular yew trees in his garden into the formal green sculpture he preferred. Although he had seen the evaporation of the hopes and ideals William Morris had instilled into Ernest Gimson and others to make furniture of good design and material for the ordinary man instead of the factory-made articles of poor design and had learnt the hard way that bringing back the old traditions of good craftsmanship was impossible because of the cost in money and time, this did

Cirencester Park gates, Cicely Street

'Pope's Seat' in Cirencester Park

not make him unduly melancholy. He was philosophic enough to enjoy the work he had done, knowing it was good, and to have a certain faith in the future.

Most of the village of Sapperton sits on a shelf, with the woods of the western limits of Cirencester Park making a rich background. There is a confusion of woodland here in both the middle and far distance, a moving arras of green, gold and russet and gleaming silver trunks. Although there is evidence of medieval and earlier ages, a sense of the eighteenth century predominates the village, in the church and in Cirencester Park. Sir Robert Atkyns once lived in the manor-house; it has been pulled down but his tomb is in the church, showing him bewigged and urbane, reclining elegantly with a book in his hand – a small book, so I suspect the sculptor never saw the elephantine folios of Sir Robert's famous *History of Gloucestershire*. It was the Atkyns family who practically rebuilt the church in classical style, using some of the secular wooden carvings from the old house as pew ends.

In the churchyard the tombs of Ernest Gimson and the Barnsley brothers lie under the trees. They have been made in the local tradition of heavy stone slabs without mouldings, with bronze plates inset into the stone giving names and dates and are like many others in the churchyard.

The tunnel entrance of the Thames and Severn Canal has an archway of dressed stone with an embattled parapet, and at the other end of the tunnel, a distance of two miles, the other entrance or exit has also a little decoration. The tunnel was dug out of solid rock, and when making it shafts were sunk about every half a mile and the stone raised on pulleys on derricks and spread around, the spoil making large tumps, which were planted with beech trees so as not to be an eyesore in the landscape and so making them a pleasant addition to the scene.

The barges propelled their craft by using their legs on the tunnel walls, and the inn at the other end of the tunnel must have been a welcome sight after two miles of strenuous legging. Norman Jewson tells a story of an old man in the village called Cainey who owned a spade guinea which he had inherited from his grandfather who happened to be near the entrance to the tunnel just after it was finished. Several gentlemen were standing on the towing path, and one of them called him and asked if he knew who he was. Cainey replied he did not, whereupon the gentleman took out a guinea and told him to look at it – and Cainey saw the face on the coin was the face of the gentleman who asked him the question. It was King George III himself, who told the old man to keep the coin to remember him by. This must have been in 1792, when the King formally opened the tunnel, and the strange thing about the episode was that so little interest seems to have been taken locally by the cottagers at least in the King's visit.

The Gimson and Barnsley tombs at Sapperton

Less than fifty years later railway engineers were superintending the making of another tunnel in the parish, about half a mile away and on a higher level. When the railway opened, the company bought up the canal and let it become derelict. They had less respect for the appearance of the countryside than the canal-makers, for the railway had come into the age of the 'muck means brass' mentality of the new industrialists pursuing progress without thought of the amenities and leaving debris in untidy heaps instead of forming it into tumps and planting them with trees so a later generation would not curse them. It was the kind of attitude that William Morris and his followers fought to overcome but it seems to have taken nearly a century to trickle through into public consciences.

At South Cerney, some three miles south of Cirencester, the Churn turns east with the old canal to go off into Wiltshire and then into the Thames. But South Cerney has other waters as well as the Churn, for disused gravel pits turned into artificial lakes are being developed for water-sports of all kinds, incidentally providing a refuge for many kinds of water-birds and plants.,

South Cerney, although close to Wiltshire, has the appearance of a true Cotswold village, as seen in a fine Norman doorway in its church, houses in the vernacular from the late seventeenth century onward and its greatest treasure, discovered in the church by a workman when restoring the tower, a fragment of a twelfth-century rood, the head and foot of a wooden crucifix described by W. R. Lethaby as 'the earliest piece of wood-carving in this country' and 'a work of great intensity'. It has a curious power to move the beholder astonishing in a piece of wood so frail, so small, that could become less than a handful of dust if a strong wind blew on it. The face of Christ has a likeness to a twelfth-century sculpture depicting the wiping of His feet by Mary Magdalen on a capital in the parish church of Stanley St Leonards; it has the same long, narrow face, deep eye sockets and drooping moustache, the face of 'a man of sorrows much acquainted with grief'. The sculpture on the capital has not been hewn out of the stone in such a way that the result is sharp and angular like so much Norman carving but is a repetition of gentle curves or rhythmic impulses. Letting oneself be drawn into its simplicity of faith produces a haunting sadness that time has robbed of its pain. It was probably hidden in the church at the Reformation to save it from being desecrated, and the covering of gesso helped to preserve it from the damp stone. Only the painted shell of the head and foot remains. The head shows a sensitive, aristocratic face, with a withdrawn expression of resignation, the work of a skilled artist who felt the sufferings of Christ so deeply that even a fragment of his work has the power to challenge the

imagination. The small foot has no blemishes, and the hole where the nail pierced has its its own poignancy.

It has been suggested the crucifix was brought back from Spain by a pilgrim wanting to enrich his own church. When I went to look at it again in June 1984, I found it had been taken to an exhibition of Romanesque art in a London Gallery, and I said a fervent prayer that it might return safely, for it is too fragile for much travelling. It has survived in its own village for the past five hundred years, and there it belongs.

The Churn is coming to the end of its life through Cotswold, but it still has a few miles of water-meadows on the last lap of its journey, and in spring this could be the most beautiful part of its meanderings. The marshy meadows of these last few miles are the home of hosts of nodding fritillaries, ragged robin, the silvery lilac of lady's smocks and all those plants that love a wet roothold, while the cuckoo shouts from the pollarded willows on its banks and the first willow wrens and chiff-chaffs sing amongst the blackthorn flowers, fragile as snow on the dark boughs.

Canal tunnel near Coates

10 · Dunt's Hamlets

Some two miles north-east of Circencester a minor road leaves Ermine Street at Stratton and goes north-west along a narrowing valley into the hills. A stream, the Dunt, a tributary of the Churn, shares the valley with a few farms, three villages and a narrow road serving them until its source at Duntisborne Abbots, where the valley comes to an end. A Saxon chief called Dunt who lived at Brimpsfield presumably owned the valley and gave his name to the stream. I was delighted to find recently that some newly planted trees by the church were whitebeams, a tree or shrub associated with the Saxons.

Daglingworth, the first village from Ermine Street, is scattered on varying heights above the stream, with the church and a big house perched on a shelf at its highest point, and one comes to it as soon as Ermine Street with its roaring traffic has been left behind, and also into a more tranquil world. The drystone walls bordering the road are decorated with stonecrop, ivy-leaved toadflax, cushioned mosses and tiny ferns, vegetation that enjoys moist valley airs and the shelter of steep hillsides. It used to be one of the earliest places in spring for finding white violets, thus making a fragrant introduction to the little valley.

In the Old Rectory gardens stands a circular pigeon-house, the only building remaining of a cell of 'superfluity' of Godstow Nunnery which held an advowson and a small pension out of the rectory of Daglingworth in the twelfth century. The pigeon-house once had 550 nest holes, so there would have been no shortage of pigeon pies for the nuns, though these rapacious birds must have been a sore trial to the neighbourhood farmers.

On the short climb to the church one passes a barn with a wide spread of roof ascending in three stages. I remember many years ago seeing two waisted waggons, the true Cotswold shape and colour, standing in front of the barn, but these have disappeared now, as has the row of horseshoes around the base of the square, plain, stone nineteenth-century Daglingworth House by the church. These small examples of the personality of residents help to give a village its own individuality in these days when conformity is overtaking us.

Evidence of the valley's Saxon origins as well as its name can be seen in the south wall of the nave, for there is long and short work at the angles and a fine Saxon sundial over the front porch. For the rest the church suffered a fierce restoration in the late nineteenth century. In the porch is an inscription in the beautiful lettering of the period:

> The Dissection and Distribution of Giles Handcox
> Who earthe bequeathe to Earthe to Heaven his Soule
> To Friends his love to the Poor a Five Pound Dole
> To remain for Ever and be Employed
> For Their Best Advantage and Reliefe
> In Daglingworth
> April 9th, 1630.

Instead of the usual twilit gloom, white walls make the interior bright and forward-looking, and there is no gloom about the Saxon carvings on the walls. David Verey, in his *Cotswold Churches*, says that 'To some people they are amongst the most moving archaic sculptures in England.' But we have to give as well as receive to feel their power. A simple piety and unquestioning faith are shown in the naïve rendering of the Christian story, with no involved symbolism to get in the way of understanding it.

The three pieces of Saxon sculpture, two in the aisle and one in the nave, were found face inward, acting as jambs of the chancel arch; the workmanship appears crude at first sight until one realizes how the sculptor has impregnated them with his own faith. In the one showing Christ in the centre, in a kilted loincloth, with a smaller figure on either side, one with a spear, the other with a sponge and jar, there is compassion as well as the whole story of the Crucifixion. The other two show St Peter with his key and Christ enthroned.

The little church has another piece of carving showing how even in the early days of church-building Cotswold masons used any piece of masonry handy rather than dig new stone from the quarry, as they have done ever since, for part of a Roman votive tablet was converted by the Saxons into a two-light window now in the wall of the modern vestry. The inscription reads: 'By Junia dedicated to the Mother Goddesses and the Genius of this place.'

Daglingworth porch with Giles's memorial and 'dissection'

Junia's Mother Goddesses and the Christian faith as the Saxons saw it and later generations interpreted it may have helped the little valley to survive unspoilt and still beautiful through many depressions and repressions of wars to a prosperous today. To those

Cotswold Bow wagon (now at Northleach Countryside Collection)

who can enjoy a pastoral scene it is a valley of small delights, satisfying to the eye and the spirit.

There is the little church of Duntisborne Rous, perfect in its setting on the green hillside with the stream below and then the woodland beyond reached by a causeway across the marshy bottom of the valley. Fortunately it did not attract the restorers, being too insignificant or remote, perhaps, or it could have been mistaken for a farm building at first sight, if one did not notice the saddlebacked tower. Its builders took advantage of the steep slope down to the stream to make a crypt under the chancel where a deeply splayed window lights a small barrel-shaped room. Its Saxon origin can be seen in a patch of herringbone masonry, long and short work at the angles and a possible fragment of Saxon sculpture high on the walls. Inside, the high, narrow nave has splendid roof timbers, wainscotting, oak pews and four misericord stalls adding the warmth of mellowed wood. The carving of vine leaves and grotesque heads on the misericords is particularly fine, and it is said that they came originally from Cirencester Abbey. Altogether the church has the look of a building cherished by those who use it. Ann Carver in her booklet published in 1968 tells the history of village and church in detail.

As I came out of the church and stood admiring the box tombs and the good lettering on the bronze nameplates, a clergyman came out of the rectory and hurried towards me. As I congratulated him on the condition of his church, he took my arm and led me to another spot in the churchyard, commanding me to look through the trees beyond the river. It was some seconds before I realized what he wanted me to see but when I gave a little gasp of surprise he smiled. 'From the smallest church on the Cotswold you can see the largest,' he pronounced. 'That is part of Cirencester church you are looking at.' He released his grip on my arm, gave a satisfied nod as of a mission accomplished and went hurriedly back to the rectory without another word. He never gave me time to thank him.

Before we come to Duntisborne Abbotts at the end of the valley, there are two more hamlets along the upper reaches of the Dunt, Leer and Middle Duntisborne, the smallest of them all. At Duntisborne Leer the stream flows almost to the doorsteps of a group of cottages so that the people who live there must have the soft lapping and babbling of its clear water as constant background music. From their front windows they can also watch the wagtails prinking and fly-catching at the water's edge. When I stopped too abruptly, they decided I was an intruder and flew off to a nearby wall, where they tittupped about, balancing their tails impatiently as they waited for me to go away.

Duntisbourne Abbotts is the largest of the Dunt villages. It also has a saddlebacked tower to its church and a splendid closing ring of late medieval date beautifully preserved, decorated with trefoils, quatrefoils and heart shapes with cross-hatching on the iron straps securing the ring to its plate. There is a similar ring at Syde only a few miles away; the same craftsman, perhaps a talented village blacksmith, was responsible for them both, or perhaps when the church belonged to the abbot of Gloucester one of the master smiths of the abbey made them, as part of his daily work.

From the water-meadows the village can be seen dotted round a small, upslanting village green or bank. From under this bank a spring gushes forth into a massive stone trough, once the village

Duntisbourne Rous Lych gate with Hobby, Martins and Starlings

115

watering place, though now the spring is tapped at its source and there is not the same fierce flow. The village now has mains water, and there is no longer gossiping about the spring while pails are being filled. It is a cool place on a hot summer day, the overflow and spray making a moist pad below the trough where mimulus and other water-plants flourish and where blackbirds and thrushes come to bathe. We used to linger there on a hot day, particularly if the continuation of our walk was south-west across the uplands to Jack Barrow crossroads where there is a road going south to Sapperton, a road on the route of an ancient trackway continuing as a metalled road to Lowesmoor Farm. The metalled road goes westward but the old track kept due south, and today all traces of it are lost in the fields.

Elkstone, Norman chancel with grotesques

11 · Blockley

Little remains today of Blockley's medieval importance as a sheep-rearing and wool-gathering centre when it belonged to the bishop of Worcester, but this early period is well documented and local historians have published a history of the parish giving the full story.

Blockley was never a town of the Staple like Chipping Campden; the sheep which produced the wool as well as the walks where they grazed belonged to the bishop, who made his own arrangements for its sale. There is, however, a record of some of Blockley's wool being sold to William Grevel of Campden, and it would appear that when the demand from the Continent became urgent, merchants bought wool where they could to meet their commitments. Like most other north Cotswold towns, Blockley declined with the wool trade and turned to agriculture until the silk-throwing trade took its place some two hundred years later to bring a new prosperity and increasing its population.

Blockley has an ancient history but a nineteenth- and twentieth-century face. Instead of the Cotswold vernacular we have the Blockley idiom, a distinctive form of it: plain, four-square houses and cottages of good ashlar with dormers but not gables, it being necessary in its narrow, steep-sided valley to build high and narrow and use every available device to increase house room. The tall, flat-fronted houses show few of the Tudor devices and are built of a local stone of an orange-buff colour, accented in some cases by a uniform wash of a deeper mustard tint. The lack of ornament or trimmings suggests the nonconformist mill-owners who built workman's cottages and other buildings in those years when Blockley was semi-industrialized. It was during this time that Blockley emerged from being an insignificant village and grew larger than its neighbour, Chipping Campden.

Most of the buildings date from the time when it was an off-shoot of Coventry's silk-throwing trade, the main source of employment. By 1780 there were five mills working along its streams, and a hundred years later some six mills employing six hundred workers, many of them children, as well as some three thousand more working in their own homes. But that industry came to an end too. A few years later the silk trade had been killed by the lifting of the tax on imported French silk ribbons into the country, and it was no longer economic to continue. Blockley tried various other ways of using its mills and water-power but it was the time of trade recessions everywhere; the piano-making, collar-making and other small industries soon died out, and the Blockley people had to find work elsewhere or tighten their belts.

In the last few decades the terraces of workers' cottages and the houses of the mill-owners and managers have been transformed into handsome residences and charming gentrified cottages; the mills along the streams, some going back to Domesday, have been turned into homes for the rich and discerning, the ponds refashioned into ornamental waters, leets into waterfalls and set about with lawns, with ornamental trees including weeping willows whose waving strands are reflected in the still waters and add greatly to the amenities of Blockley's new grace, a one-time scene of industry turned into a pleasance.

Blockley is a good example of how to put the depressing remains of a lost industry to good use by turning them into a considerable financial asset and giving the village a charm it never possessed before. It has taken on an aspect of rural peace – one could almost say innocence – with its clear, shallow stream overhung by willows, its ducks paddling by. It has also become garden-conscious and has two flower shows a year to give its residents the opportunity of competing with its neighbours in friendly fashion. Owing to its position in a ravine in the hills there is only a narrow road with an elevated footpath to keep pedestrians from being mown down or entangled in traffic, so gardens must be at the back of the houses on rising ground and frontages satisfied with a narrow edging of plants climbing the house walls. This they do with great luxuriance, while from the walls themselves are hung baskets filled with red and pink geraniums, blue lobelias, fuchsias, petunias and other flowering plants, so that all summer long, as one goes towards the woods of Dovedale, Blockley looks *en fête* and one feels there should be band music in the background.

The village is on several levels, which gives another interest, so

one must climb up and down short bursts of steep paths to get to know it, and this produces fascinating vistas of roofs of varying heights. The lowest level has the stream with tree-shaded gardens coming down to the water with its mimulus, iris and other water-plants; the second level holds the church, the High Street and the road to the woods, and then after another steep climb the top road leading out into the wolds and those fields that were once the bishop of Worcester's sheep-walks.

Aston Magna lies some two miles north-east of Blockley and was closely associated with it in the days when the district was under the ecclesiastical rule of Worcester, but it shows no signs today that it benefited from this ownership. There is a shell of medieval building in one of the farmhouses, probably the remains of a chapel used by the bishop or his stewards on their yearly visits to collect wool from the many thousands of sheep that once grazed the sheep-walks above the villages.

The village consists mainly of one long street with some pleasant stone houses and terraces of cottages. It was one of the villages where the farmers did not move out in the eighteenth century and built themselves houses apart in their fields to signify their right to be considered minor gentry in that very class-conscious age. As one goes down the village street towards where the valley widens into fields, its appearance deteriorates. The gaunt walls of a large, roofless barn with a heap of scrap at its feet, blackened by a disastrous fire, are a desolate sight and cast a gloom over this stretch of the street. On the opposite side of the railway bridge in a dip in the watery meadows, and opposite a large village green bordered by a modern housing estate, stands a disused church in an unkempt churchyard. David Verey in his book on Cotswold churches calls it a 'rather mean building'. Probably in the days when it had a congregation and was cherished as a parish church it appeared more graceful; today it is a desolate sight, unwanted, unloved. It makes a depressing approach to the village if one comes to it from a small road leading off the Foss.

Dorn, now a hamlet in the same confluence of tiny streams that made up Knee Brook, is less than a quarter of a mile from the Foss but feels curiously remote, as if it still belonged to the past or had not yet caught up with the present. It was once a considerable Roman settlement, and large numbers of Roman coins, funerary

Village street, Blockley

stones and altars have been found in the district, though it has not been professionally excavated. 'Dorn' is a British name and means a gated stronghold; from its position just off the Foss it could have been a military post. Without proper excavation it is impossible to do more than conjecture.

Ditchford and Upton, two other settlements in the neighbourhood, have been lost villages since the Middle Ages; they may have been deserted to make way for sheep-walks when only a few shepherds were required instead of the usual band of ploughmen, carters and other farm workers and so fell into disuse. Both villages seem to have been lost before the Black Death.

Evidence of Roman occupation has been found about Upton also. Upton Wold farmhouse, a mile west of Blockley, is a characteristic Cotswold seventeenth-century manor-house of three gables, a three-storeyed porch having rusticated ovals, mullioned windows with labels descending in the correct order to the ground floor. It has a flat-arched moulded stone doorway and stone chimneys set diagonally, a perfect example for the textbooks, but one feels it should be in a populous village with all the accompaniments, a church, a rectory, cottages and the other things that once made up a Cotswold village.

12 · Winchcombe and Hailes

Winchcombe has its own river, the Isbourne, which rises about half a mile from the source of the Coln near Sevenhampton but unlike the Coln flows north into the Warwickshire Avon. Local folklore says that rivers that 'run against the sun' have special qualities, and this is true of the Isbourne, for its waters are free from iron, thus making them suitable for making fine filter papers used in hospitals and laboratories. The Isbourne has served Winchcombe well in the past, providing the power for mills, iron foundries, tanneries and other small industries.

From 1752 the main source of employment was the Postlip Mills, and the life of the little town practically depended upon them, the owners being paternally inclined to their workpeople and providing almshouses, cottages, means of recreation, schooling and other benefits. The mills are still operating today and still making special filter papers, but the largest mill reservoir which once provided the water power is now an ornamental lake bordered with reeds and osiers and the home of waterfowl, giving the scene the tranquillity only a sheet of quiet water can provide. The old drying shed with its wooden-slatted openings has disappeared; the slats were adjusted to let in sufficient air to dry the paper properly, and setting the openings so that the right amount of air went through the building and dried out the paper at the proper speed must have needed skill and experience not available today.

In the early 1900s bands of travelling basket-makers used to camp out on the river's banks, cutting the osiers and so keeping the heads of the pollarded willows from growing topheavy. The withies were made into the large baskets used for carrying rags, paper and pulp about the mill. Then, when they had made the required number of baskets the workers were off on their travels again. In her *The Short History of Postlip Mills*, Eleanor Adlard, a member of the family who

Gargoyles around Winchcombe Church

owned the mills, tells how the local people regarded these travelling people and used them to warn naughty children that the basket-makers would get them if they did not behave, but I doubt if they were as scared of them as their ancestors were of the travelling people who processed the woad at Wadfield, according to Celia Fiennes who describes meeting them on one of her seventeenth-century journeys through the country. Like the reddlemen, the woad-men carried the marks of their trade on their persons as well as on their clothes, and as the dye, or mordant, was of a dingy dark blue, their aspect could be frightening enough for them to be used as bogey-men by mothers to quell unruly children.

Taking a casual stroll through Winchcombe, one finds it difficult to believe it was once the seat of Mercian royalty and that an important abbey flourished here, bringing princes and nobles to worship at the sacred shrine and to conduct the affairs of the Mercian ascendancy in its brief period of political stability. Winchcombe was also a borough – that is, a town inhabited by free tradesmen, free craftsmen and free burgesses, not by serfs liable for labour on their lord's demesne. A record contemporary with Domesday gives the

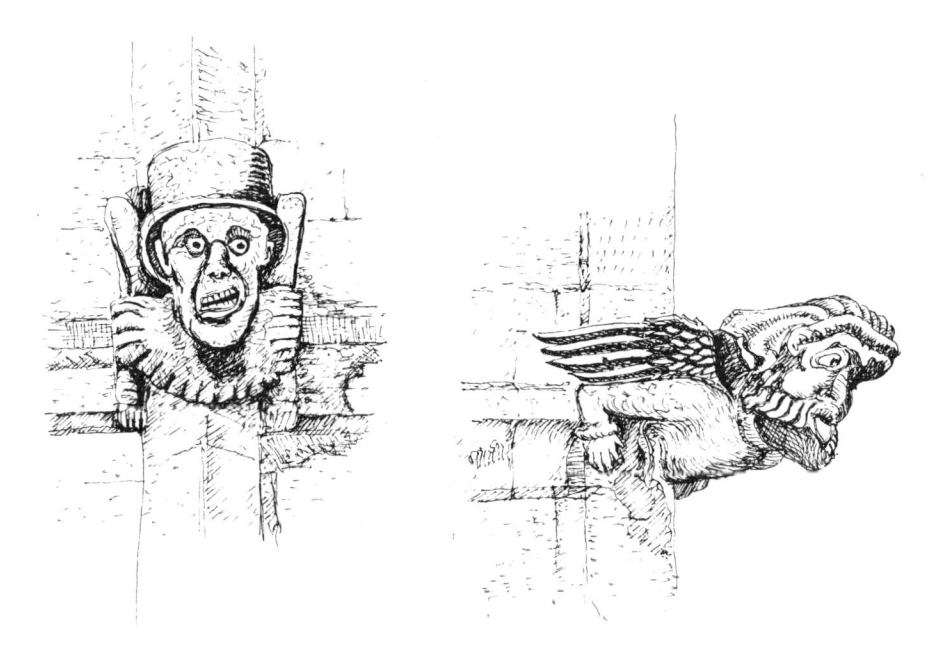

number of burgesses as 151, and adding their wives, children and dependents this would be considered a town in those days. Professor Finburg states that its 'urban origin' dates from the Anglo-Saxon period. Before then Winchcombe's 'fat valley', as the Romans called it, held Wadfield villa, overlooking Beesmoor Brook, Spoonley Wood villa and Stancombe Wood villa, which has been vandalized and never properly excavated. East of Spoonley Wood runs the White Way, providing a well-used track to Corinium, a cultural centre as well as a place where the Romano-British went to pay their taxes and to enjoy the pleasures of an urban centre with its forum, baths and shops.

The church of St Peter's was built in 1465 by the abbot of Winchcombe, who wanted the townspeople to have their own church because of the many quarrels between the monks and the town, the townspeople erecting the nave with the aid of Sir Ralph Botelier of Sudeley Castle before he was disgraced by the defeat of the Lancastrians in 1469. It was a new church designed in the Perpendicular style in fashion at the time, its special feature a fine set of gargoyles showing how the masons of Winchcombe were following the traditions of good craftsmanship laid down by Richard of Winch-combe, master mason, who was responsible for the Oxford University School of Divinity early in the fifteenth century.

The arguments between the town and the monks do not seem to have been settled by the building of a parish church, for it is recorded that the monks appealed to the Pope to stop the townspeople ringing their bells during the abbey's services. The gargoyles played their part in the disagreements between the two factions, and the towns-people liked to explain that the grotesque heads were caricatures of the monks who had offended them. Winchcombe people's habit of naming the gargoyles after people they disliked returned in the 1914–1918 war when one head, because of its fierce mustachios, was nicknamed 'Kaiser Bill'. There is something to be said of having an image of an enemy to revile; nobody is hurt and it gets rid of a lot of bile. Cotsallers, like many countrymen, have a genius for acid comment when they are powerless to retaliate in any other way.

Since it lost its abbey, Winchcombe has always come second to Sudeley in importance, today getting only a small proportion of the tourist trade, as one can see by watching the coaches roll by on their way to the many attractions the castle offers to visitors, few of them having anything to do with the history of the place. The day I like to imagine when I visit Sudeley is the one when Queen Elizabeth I came here on one of her progresses. At the gate of the castle she was greeted by a shepherd in a snow-white smock holding his crook and bowing low. Part of his speech has come down to us, and it would be nice to know if it was extempore or written by a scribe belonging to the castle and then the likeliest shepherd chosen to recite it. I also hope it was a real shepherd and not a courtier dressed as one, for the words have an honest ring: 'Your Highness is come unto Cotswold, an uneven country, but people that carry their thoughts level with their fortune . . . The hills present nothing but cottages and nothing can we present to your Highness but this lock of wool, Cotswold her fruit and my poor gift I offer to your Highness in which nothing is esteemed but the whiteness, Virginity's colour, nor to be expected but duty, shepherd's religion.' It is interesting that Sudeley's shepherd should use the same word as Shakespeare for the hills he called 'those rough uneven ways', so evidently in Elizabeth's time the word 'uneven' had this meaning.

Winchcombe, however, has its own quiet charm amid the greater

Gallery in The George, Winchcombe

charm of its setting of wooded hillsides and green meadows. There is an ancient inn, 'The George', said to have been used by pilgrims to the abbey and built before 1525, for on the spandrels to its doorway are the initials of Richard Kidderminster, the Abbot of Winchcombe, who was chosen by the King to preach a stern warning sermon on heresy, though it was said that the object was to point out to the Commons and the King that the immunity of the clergy from Common Law was absolute. It set off a controversy that came to an end only when Henry VIII declared: 'We are, by sufference of God, King of England and in time past never had any superior but God', a speech that presaged the end of the Pope's rule in England and the end of the great religious houses which owned such a large part of the country. Being a politician as well as head of a great abbey, Abbot Kidderminster even then felt the cold wind blowing and feared for the future.

The little town has known violent fluctuations in prosperity and dire poverty. The wool trade does not seem to have brought much wealth to the town, though it certainly enriched the abbeys of Winchcombe and Hailes. After the Dissolution, with the monks gone who had cared for the sick and the poor, it tried many other ways to make a living. It was at this time that Leland called it a place 'where a few poore houses be'. Tobacco-growing flourished for a short period, and it seemed as if at last Winchcombe had found the right occupation, for the records of John Stratford, the instigator of tobacco-growing there, show he paid out on wages £1,400 in one year, and calculated in the wages at the time this meant that two hundred or more people were employed planting and tending the crop. But heedless of the needs of an impoverished area, tobacco-growing was made illegal in England (King Charles wanting to encourage the Virginian planters). Governments do not seem to have changed much down the centuries. Pepys in his diary gives vivid accounts of the men of Winchcombe's fights with the soldiers sent to destroy their crops, but by 1690 tobacco-growing had died out, helped by the fact that the American colonies were selling their tobacco so cheaply that it was no longer economic to grow it in England.

During the Civil Wars Winchcombe suffered under the Royalist forces of Sir Henry Bard. In an edition of Parliamentary Papers of 5 April 1643, an entry runs: 'I fear the way is something dangerous from Warwick to Gloucester. Some of Campden's garrison went lately to Winchcombe, where they plundered them so there was not a Sunday shift of clothes left them. All the cattle drove away.' Up to that time Sudeley Castle had provided some work, though from the first it was a case of 'the rich man in his castle, the poor man at his gate', but on 29 September 1649 the Council of State reported that the castle had been rendered useless for military purposes. It stood desolate, growing more ruinous as time went by, and for nearly two hundred years was a free-for-all quarry, inhabited by the squatters of that age, Katherine Parr's tomb desecrated, its former glory become a folktale.

The famines of the Napoleonic Wars, at the beginning of the nineteenth century, were another setback but it could not have been all disastrous living for there was work to be had in the paper-mills, and the population continued to grow though not as quickly as in other towns in the county. At the beginning of the 1840s Winchcombe was a poor, isolated backwater while Cheltenham, once the smaller town, had begun to flourish. The Dent family, wealthy glove-makers of Worcester looking for the prestige of a country seat, bought Sudeley Castle and its estate and quickly proceeded to restore it. With this interest in the welfare of the town and ability to provide work and help in other ways such as schooling, Winchcombe began to prosper again. Since then it has never looked back, resolving into the quiet, grey little town it is today, a good shopping centre with many interests of its own. Because of its nearness to Cheltenham, it has been increased by commuters but they in their turn have brought many diverse interests and activities to the town, so that it has its own life and need not depend on Cheltenham for its entertainments.

Less than two miles north-east of Winchcombe the remains of Hailes Abbey stand in a quiet meadow under a sloping hillside that shelters it from the east winds. It was founded in 1246 by Richard of Cornwall, Henry III's younger brother, as a thank-offering for escaping drowning in a shipwreck. Nothing remains of the buildings today but the foundations, a few fragments of cloister arches and such pieces of carved stone and broken pillars as remained after it was demolished and the ruins used by the village as a quarry for several hundred years. The uncovered foundations are laid out in a spacious, dignified setting which makes one understand how large an establishment it must have been, under the hillside where the monks had a vineyard and where the ancient Salt Way climbs to Farmcote and then on to a meeting of tracks at Roel Gate. There is a small museum displaying carved bosses from a vaulted ceiling and other finds and relics of the abbey, and outside a pleasant forecourt

Hailes Abbey, museum details

with pieces of carved stones, cornices, pillars and capitals showing what a magnificent abbey it must have been and how skilful were its masons and sculptors. There are six bosses in the museum that are marvellous examples of stiff-leaf ornament and undercutting; in one of Christ rending the jaws of Satan one can feel the force in every carved muscle. The exhibits have been found in excavations that each season add a little to one's knowledge of the buildings and the life of the monks who lived in them.

Before the National Trust took over, the ruins were more mysterious and romantic-looking, like a scene in a Gothic novel. Dark trees and rough vegetation pressed about them so that under lowering skies in the gloom of evening one imagined that some of the despair and heartbreak felt by the monks in losing their home and seeing it violated still lingered there. But I prefer the ruins open to the light and air. One gets a truer conception of its size and can imagine how it must have looked when Henry III with Queen Eleanor and the court came riding from Winchcombe for its dedication in 1251, when there was 'a great gathering of Kings and Queens and temporal Great Ones of England' forming a procession to worship in the vast new abbey church. In documents of the time it is described as a 'scene of surpassing splendour', and so it must have been.

The abbey had many benefactors who gave lavishly that they might benefit by the monks' prayers, and at the Dissolution it owned thirteen thousand acres of land. The famous relic 'the blode of Christ that is in Hayle' brought pilgrims and their gifts from all over the country. Cistercians knew about sheep and how to make good use of the sheep-walks that came to them, for they were an order skilled in sheep-breeding and improving the quality of wools, and they must have improved the breeds of Cotswold sheep by selling their rams outside their own manors as well as within them.

With two abbeys so close to each other, the people of Winchcombe and neighbourhood were well looked after. We know something of Winchcombe's quarrelling with monks of Winchcombe Abbey because of the Papal Bulls still in existence, for they applied to the Pope with petty complaints – at least they seem petty today. Hailes leaves no record that her monks behaved in this way, perhaps because there was the little church at the abbey gates for pilgrims, thus keeping the abbey church for the monks.

The abbey's passing also seems to have been attended by less trouble for the King and the men he used for the job of pulling the religious houses down. The abbot and his monks accepted pensions, and at least three found posts as parish priests at Longborough, Didbrook and Far Pinnock. The abbot, an astute politician in touch with affairs of state, seeing the way the wind was blowing, trimmed his sails accordingly, doing the best he could for himself and his men as he realized it was useless to fight the authority of the King. His temporal power, once so widespread, had been shattered and his spiritual power outmoded by the new Protestant spirit of the times. It befitted men of God to submit, but it could not have been easy. As usual it was the aged poor, the sick and the workless who suffered most, for the monks had been generous dole-givers, and suddenly they were no more.

In this tranquil setting one does not feel the sorrow, dismay and bitterness that must have been in the hearts of many when they saw the abbey in ruins. It must have been a shock also to the schools of masons and other craftsmen belonging to the abbey who lost their livelihoods and their homes. Their dispersal undoubtedly benefited the outside world in the long run by an eruption of trained craftsmen, and it could have been responsible for the good building traditions that make Cotswold famous today, for excellence of work was the criterion in the monasteries and abbeys, only the best being acceptable for a house of God. There was time and opportunity to develop, contact with Continental ideas and no need to worry where the next job or meal was coming from. These men handed down their knowledge and strict terms of apprenticeship, which finally made the rules of a 'mistery' that was almost a religion in itself. Many must have found work with the new masters of the estates that once belonged to the abbey or in the stoneyards and workships of the King, for good craftsmen rarely lack good masters. The masons were well-organized and looked after their own, as well as ensuring that the secular work was of the same high order as the work they did for the great religious houses.

13 · Cutsdean to Cogges by River

The Windrush begins its thirty-mile journey to the Thames as a spring bubbling out of the hillside near Cutsdean or, in a dry summer, as a damp patch with barely enough moisture to quench the thirst of a butterfly or wandering beetle. It was a couple of white butterflies which helped me find the source by their hovering over a few drops of water hanging on the grass of the field. This is windy country of isolated farms and roads that before the war were gated tracks, good walking with wide-spreading views for those who enjoy solitude, and though not much more than seven hundred feet up, it feels much nearer the sky. Even in these days, when one is beginning to feel there are no lonely places left to refresh the spirit, one can find peace and solitude high on Cotswold, though a main road or village may be only a mile or so away.

Ford has an inn now known beyond the surrounding district for it caters for tourists. In the old days it was patronized mostly by local people, and the occasional walker who dropped in could feel out of it listening to the talk of barley prices and the iniquities of the government towards farmers, but it was a valuable port of call on a thirsty day, though I remember years ago sitting there with tears streaming down my cheeks as an elderly farmworker tackled his lunch of bread, bacon and a large onion, my companion amused at the onion's effect upon me. Looking back, it is not always the poetic moments one remembers about walks on Cotswold.

In another mile Windrush comes to Temple Guiting, and many springs gushing out of its banks turn it into a river. Temple Guiting once belonged to the Knights Templars, who had a fulling-mill here in 1182, one of the earliest in the country; at a time when England's main export was wool and not cloth, the records say that the Templars' was not the coarse cloth woven for home use but a finer variety made especially for export. Above the river and the road is

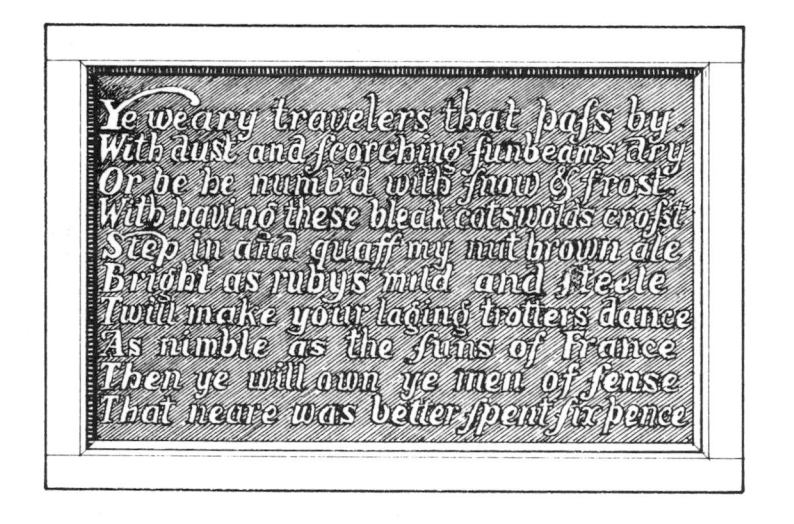

Ye weary travelers that pass by.
With dust and scorching sunbeams dry
Or be he numb'd with snow & frost.
With having these bleak cotswolds crost
Step in and quaff my nut brown ale
Bright as rubys mild and steele
Twill make your laging trotters dance
As nimble as the suns of France
Then ye will own ye men of sense
That neare was better spent sixpence

Ford village and sign at The Plough

Manor Farmhouse, one of the finest small Elizabethan houses on Cotswold, with two gables, buttresses, mullioned windows having four-centred arched heads, and a dovecot built onto the house itself, with nests for 2,500 birds. It once had a great hall open to the roof, as smoke-blackened timbers testify. There have been many alterations inside the house, and in odd corners and cupboards traces of the old winding stairs can be found. It is believed to have been the country home of a bishop of Worcester. It is not easy to see – indeed, Temple Guiting itself is not easy to see as a whole because of the different levels and the tree-shaded lanes that suggest a kind of secretiveness so that one can go through the village without knowing one has done so.

Frances Witt describes Temple Guiting House, as he saw it in 1827, and tells how tastefully the grounds were laid out: the plantations, the meadows with haymakers, 'groves cool and umbrageous', the lawns dotted with single trees, and 'the grotto cold and dark all bespeaking good taste and opulence'. Alas, the grotto cool and dark has disappeared.

When Mr Talbot, who lived at Temple Guiting House, died in 1836, his celebrated flock of Southdown sheep were sold, people coming from all over the country to bid for them, showing that after the Knights Templars had fulled their cloth made from the wool of Cotswold sheep landowners had continued to improve breeds which had taken the place of the old Cotswold 'lions'. Francis Witt described these sheep as 'of exquisite symmetry', praise indeed from one who was chary of praise or any kind of extravagant remark.

The Windrush comes to Guiting Power, a village much decayed in the first half of the twentieth century but now reborn by judicious renovating and building. The cottages around the sloping village green have not been over-gentrified or had the vernacular over-stressed; new houses of good quality are strung out along the road at the entrance to the village; there is a pleasant village hall used by the villagers, and each year they hold a little musical festival and exhibitions of the work of local artists.

By the time the river comes to Naunton, it is fullgrown and enters fully into the village scene, yet Naunton keeps the feeling of an upland village although most of the cottages are on a road following the river with only narrow meadowland between it and the water. I like to look down on Naunton from above – not too far above, so there is only a huddle of roofs and chimneys to be seen, but at a place where the river winding between rushy banks can be seen just

Naunton

as it is disappearing under Harford Bridge, having the skyline as
backcloth for its old grey houses that turn silvery in the slanting light
of evening with the river reflecting the skyglow in its placid waters.
It is then I wonder why Cobbett said of the Windrush that it was
'poor, dull and uninteresting'.

Naunton, like Aylworth and Harford, was a full-sized village at
the time of Domesday, but monastic landlords in the fifteenth century
specialized in sheep-rearing and the number of inhabitants conse-
quently declined, as they did when the Knights Templars were the
landlords a hundred years earlier at Harford. Wool so helpful to the
country's exchequer was also the ruin of many a village: 'Where
forty persons had their living, now one man and his shepherd hath
all,' wrote Sir Thomas More in the early sixteenth century. He saw
the sheep as a monster devouring not only the landless peasant but
England herself: 'Your sheep that were wont to be so meek and tame

and so small eaters now . . . become so great devourers that they eat up and swallow the very men themselves.' But the warnings of prophets are rarely heeded, and the end of the fifteenth century saw England largely a nation of sheep-farmers, with the making of cloth beginning to take over. It was at this prosperous period that Naunton's stone pulpit was made, one of the few stone pulpits on Cotswold with its miniature canopies, traceries and pinnacled buttresses carved by a master hand.

The Windrush provides the town's pleasure area at Bourton-on-the-Water after it has flowed under Bourton Bridge and come to the little bridges and lawns over channels of clear water where ducks bask in the admiration of visitors and wait for their doles. Soon after leaving Bourton it is joined by the Dikler and the Eye brook to meander through meadows on its way to Oxfordshire. Great Barrington and Taynton, two villages on its way, were famous for their quarries of fine-quality stone in the seventeenth and eighteenth centuries.

At Great Barrington there is Barrington Park, a Palladian mansion erected for Lord Chancellor Talbot after the sixteenth-century manor-house was burnt down. It was built on a natural terrace overlooking the river, which was then diverted into an ornamental lake crossed by a delightful three-arched bridge. The gardens were landscaped after the fashion of the period and adorned with a small domed Roman temple and a pigeon house, attributed to Kent. The temple can be seen through fine but rusting railings with stone piers and ball finials, making a charming picture in the spacious park dotted with single trees of magnificent proportions. The Manor Farm has two large barns with classical ornament. Barrington Park must have been one of the most elegant houses on Cotswold when it was kept in the grand fashion of the day, but both the mansion and the village have a sad, deserted look today. The story of its decline is a dolorous one.

> Remote from folly and from wit
> Here pensive fancy loves to sit
> Midst the soft surrounding scene,

wrote Barrington Park's gentle tame poet Thomas More, who, in the manner of impecunious poets in that age of patronage, sang for his supper to amuse the noble company assembled there as guests of Lord Talbot.

Perhaps even sadder than Barrington Park is the sculptured monu-

Bourton Bridge over the Windrush on the Foss Way

Great Barrington, view of the temple through the gates

ment in the church to two children of the Bray family who died of smallpox. The boy, who in the fifteenth year of his age died on Christmas Day 1720, wears a square braided coat and the cravat and peruke of the period, and he holds his sister Jane by the hand. 'The beauties of his person were equal to those of his mind,' we are told. Jane, who was eight when she died, is dressed as for a ball in a tight-bodiced gown with full brocaded skirts. The two figures are escorted by a guardian angel, a figure of power and dignity whose protecting wings overshadow the children. The boy's eyes are fixed on the angel as if for reassurance, while Jane is half turned, looking backward as they walk among the heavenly clouds. Kathleen Esdaile,

139

in *English Church Monuments*, deduced that it was made by Francis Bird, Christopher Wren's favourite sculptor, who made the monument for Wren's own beloved daughter in St Paul's.

Little Barrington is a far happier place, its cottages standing round the rim of a shallow bowl which was once a quarry from which the stone to build them was taken. It is open to every breeze, and sometimes the blue of the sky is glimpsed in the water of a spring coming out of the side of the bowl to make a bright green ribbon winding across it and then across a field to join the Windrush. Each cottage has some small distinguishing feature setting it apart from the others, a different kind of head-mould, a dormer, a stone porch and so on, and this gives a pleasing artlessness to the collection. Contrivance could not have produced such a happy result. Before the cottages had water laid on, and when local farmworkers lived in them, the scene could become one of biblical simplicity when the cottagers came to the spring for water with their buckets and ewers, particularly when in cold weather they were wrapped in old-fashioned long coats, with shawls wrapped about their heads. It was an opportunity for gossip, and many a titbit of scandal would be gone over while the buckets filled. The necessities of life are the same in the Far East as in Little Barrington, and in this small fold in the hills when I was young, women in long pinafores standing in groups waiting their turn at the spring were akin to those in my picturebook of Bible stories.

Windrush village, despite being named after the river, does not seem as much a riverside village as others the river passes on its way through Cotswold. The village street is raised well above the water-meadows, its church higher still, and its quarries of excellent freestone including a mine are a little way out of the village on the hillside and not easy to find today. The sloping little green is planted with lime trees, and there is a stone mounting-block by the churchyard wall used in the days when many of the local farmers rode to church with their wives behind on the pillion.

From the moment one enters the churchyard, one knows this is a place where good masons, monumental and otherwise, have left their mark, for on the two bale tombs the ends have a horned sheep instead of the usual cherub, shell or quatrefoil, while inside a formalized ram's head adorns the place where an arch begins to spring from its pillar. The south doorway is one of the best Norman doorways on

Norman door at Windrush Church

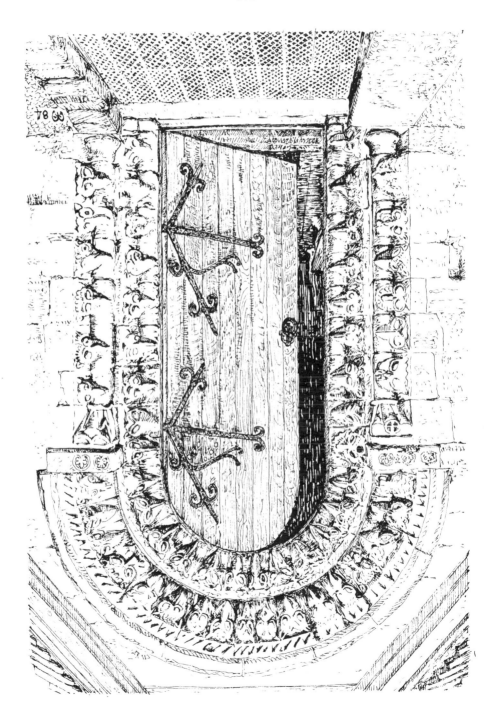

Cotswold, and looking at it just after thinking about the ram's head the double row of fantastic beakheads have just that same bony ridge, the great oval protruding eyes of some kind of monstrous sheep. Inside, the chancel is faced in dressed stone, very pleasing in its simplicity. Indeed, there is a completeness of workmanship about the church and its churchyards in the work of all its periods that delights the eye and the mind, and this includes a carved Jacobean pulpit, one of the finest of its kind on Cotswold and which shows to advantage in the plain, light interior.

The Sherborne brook rises in the Northleach wolds near Farmington, where its springs once supplied the village pump on the green. The brook accompanies the road to Sherborne until it comes to the village, when it goes winding north-west to join the Windrush. Despite its short life, it is no trickling stream but free-running, with ash and willow, those loveliest of riverside trees, on its banks, and poplar and aspen, whose foliage makes shimmers of silver amid the darker foliage of hawthorn and wych elm.

Sherborne Manor once belonged to Winchcombe Abbey, and the abbots at shearing time in May would come with their household and stay a month, superintending the collection of the wool and, I expect, enjoying the scene. Sherborne was one of the abbey's richest manors and capable of providing the extra food and fodder necessary for this annual influx, while the broad, flat valley provided the space for marshalling the thousands of sheep and the wide, shallow brook had the pools for washing them. Sherborne was not far from the main road to London and the wool-mart of Northleach where merchants came to bargain for the packed wool. R. H. Hilton wrote in *Gloucestershire Studies* that in 1488 fourteen hundred sheep were washed and shorn and the fleeces folded by hired labour, while the bulk of the work was done by the cottagers who owed 12½ days washing and shearing to the abbey, as well as sewing up the wool in packs of two hundred fleeces ready for transport. When the shearing was over, there was the sheep-shearing festival in which everybody joined. There was dancing and feasting as well as prayers, a reward for the village for a month of hard work by them all.

A cottage with a simple Norman archway and two small Early English windows may have belonged to a chapel of ease for the abbot on his visits to Sherborne. After the Dissolution Sherborne House belonged to John Dutton, a wealthy wool-man who had friends at court because of his wealth, but soon after he took over Sherborne House it was burnt down. It was another member of the family,

Thomas Dutton, who built the almshouses for women in Northleach in 1616.

The family built the present mansion at Sherborne in 1850, and the great high wall that shuts in the house and its grounds and stretches along almost a mile of the village street, a splendid if forbidding piece of masonry. It is said it was built to give work to unemployed of the neighbourhood at a time when there was much poverty. The landowners and rich farmers, having to supply a meagre dole to keep the villagers from starving, found giving the unemployed such work a way of getting some return for their Relief as well as keeping the men occupied, as idle, hungry men can get into mischief.

Soon after leaving Sherborne the brook joins the Windrush, and the river then flows gently in loops and double loops past Windrush village and Little Barrington on one side and Great Barrington and Taynton on the other as it comes through the willow-hung water-meadows to Burford.

In this age, when all places tend to look alike, Burford has kept its individuality; indeed, it is stronger than ever it was, for it has at last realized that its distinction is worth cultivating. One could never mistake the little town for anywhere else. It is partly its setting, with the old stone bridge over the river and the church at its feet, the march of the steep, wide road with, at the upper end, an avenue of round-headed trees as it comes to open Cotswold at the top, the variety of the buildings that line the street, the way other streets go off at right angles, showing glimpses of interesting stone houses and then the open countryside, with no sprawl and litter on its fringes spoiling the whole.

There are roofs of all sizes and elevations; some have dormers, others are steep-pitched Tudor style, and a few belonging to the larger, more imposing houses, several of them designed and built by Christopher Kempster, have parapets and pediments setting off the plain rectangles of their façade. Windows vary, from those with stone mullions and transoms to sash windows wide or narrow, and the doorways not belonging to the shops range from narrow openings or archways just big enough to take a loaded packmule to the tall, wide archways big enough for a loaded coach to enter the court of an inn. Early Tudor to classical frontages, Victorian, Edwardian and nondescript blend together because of the quality of their building stone where even the antique grey of the ancient fronts keeps a gleam of their original gold, while the darker grey of the stone-tiled roofs makes the proper climax. There is also a general feeling of well-being

Monumental Tomb, Burford Church
to Edmund Harman Esq. 1569.

which has come to Burford now that a prosperous tourist trade has taken it out of the doldrums of the beginning of the century. It is also a shopping town for the villages around.

And if the purists complain that Burford exists mainly for visitors, the reply is that it was always a place where travellers on the way to the west or Oxford or London stopped for refreshment from its earliest days when a ford was the only way of crossing the Windrush and when the medieval bridge was built and then kept in repair by wool-men donating the money as an act of piety and because they must have known the rigours of travel in those early days. Later still, during the coaching era, dozens of coaches stopped at Burford daily, though they did not drive straight up the hill but went by way of Witney Street to avoid the steep climb. They included the coaches of Thomas Haines Junior who operated from the Royal Hotel, Cheltenham, every day but Sunday, and whose fly-waggons went through Northleach, Burford, Witney, Oxford and Wycombe to the Blossoms Inn, Cheapside, in London, taking two days on the journey. The names of the coaches were an indication of the kind of country they traversed, the hunting country about Burford and Chipping Norton and between Oxford and Birmingham: they were named *Nimrod*, *Tallyho*, *Harkaway* and *Tantivy*, while the *Defiance*, *Revenge*, *Self-Defence* and *Retaliator* told of the competition between the various companies, though I wonder if the *Annihilator* seemed an ominous name to its passengers. Diaries and letters of that period make bitter play on the names of the coaches, just as railway passengers did in the railway age with the initials of the companies, like Slow and Dirty for the Somerset and Dorset. The *Magnet*, wrote one passenger, was without attraction, the *Regulator* uncertain, the *Flyer* crawled and so on. One must remember that the earlier coaches had no springs and that the condition of the roads was atrocious.

When the coaching era ended, Burford lost most of its income and the citizens awoke to the fact that they had behaved foolishly over the Enclosure Act, not looking to the future but taking the petty recompense offered by the attorneys of the big landowners so that their common fields were lost to them for ever, and they no longer had any place to graze their cows, geese and sheep.

Burford was famous for its saddles, but this was specialist work and the demand was small. One was presented to Charles II when he came to the races, costing the burgesses £21, while cleansing the

Burford, the Harman tomb

streets when His Majesty came through cost only two shillings. William III also came to the town and was given a saddle, but there is no record that the streets were cleansed for him, though one hopes they were. He and his retinue were probably served with a Burford Bait, a gargantuan meal consisting mostly of the venison for which Burford was famous at that time because its association with Wychwood Forest allowed its people a certain amount of free hunting there. When the privilege was taken away from them, they went poaching, and the carcases of the deer were hidden in the bale tombs of the churchyard, but I do not think the merchants who rested there would have objected, for they had probably enjoyed many a Burford Bait from deer they had poached themselves.

The few miles between Burford and Swinbrook are the most serene of the Oxford reaches of the Windrush, with a quiet road meandering beside it above flood-level edged with low stone walls so one can see the willows marking the river all the way. Widford is nothing but the tiny church of St Oswold, standing on the site of a Roman villa and with part of its tessellated pavement paving the chancel, though whether this was ignorance, economy or because the builders found it too difficult to break up the Roman cement we do not know. At Woodchester grave-diggers in the eighteenth century, when all memory or traditions of a Roman settlement on the spot had faded, found it difficult to dig deeply because of the famous Roman pavement long buried in accumulations of soil being embedded in a cement of adamantine hardness. We do not know what happened to the village to leave the little church alone in a meadow.

Swinbrook, the next village on the Windrush, was the home of the Fettiplaces who, as the rhyme says, with the Traceys and the Laceys owned all the best manors, parks and chases. The last of the family died in 1803 and their mansion has disappeared; no one could tell me where it used to stand, as if the local people wanted to forget them, for tradition says their rule was cruel and overbearing.

The Resedales acquired most of Swinbrook and Widford at the beginning of the nineteenth century but their holdings were sold in 1926, and in 1958 the family ceased to be officially connected with the parish. There are memorials to members of the family in the church and churchyard.

The most elaborate memorials, however, are to the Fettiplace family, the earliest, a brass of 1510 before the altar, of the Anthony

The Old Vicarage, High Street, Burford

147

who was the founder of the Swinbrook branch of the family. The north wall of the chancel was recessed to hold the extraordinary two-tiered monuments of the Fettiplaces of the sixteenth and seventeenth centuries, erected by Sir Edmund Fettiplace, and the effigies represent his grandfather, his father and himself. He died in 1613. The two sculptors commissioned to make the monuments were obliged to exercise their ingenuity to fit them into the prescribed space. There being no room to make recumbent figures and wanting to show the figures in full armour, the sculptors displayed them reclining on an elbow, one hand resting on an elaborately chased sword, the other supporting the head. The posture is repeated in each tier, with small differences in hair, dress and armour because of the years between the two groups. There is nothing to suggest the solemnity of death, the lifelike postures suggesting they were taking their ease with an elegant arrogance befitting their position. An unknown Burford sculptor made one of them, and William Byrd of Oxford the other, but in both the work is of high quality, their detail meticulous. The Fettiplace mansion is lost, the memory of their lordship over the place forgotten but the work of the Burford and Oxford craftsman remains to delight us. A more conventional eighteenth-century memorial records the death of Sir George Fettiplace in 1743, the last holder of the title.

In the churchyard are several bale tombs, for this is still the area of the Burford masons, and the idea has been put forward that this type of tomb was invented by Timothy Strong, quarryman and mason of Great Barrington, whose son and grandson helped to build St Paul's. Knowing the Cotsaller's passion for making everything possible of stone caused me to wonder if the theory that the bale shape represented corded packs of wool might not be a later interpretation and if the other theory might be more plausible – that they represent the iron framework erected over biers and coffins over which a handsome pall was hung when an important personage was being carried to the last resting place. A master mason such as Timothy Strong could have seen such a burial of a nobleman when he was employed in London and been inspired to create such a design on the top of a table tomb for less exalted clients. Although an occasional bale tomb is found outside the Burford area, most are found in the churchyards of the villages of the Windrush from Burford onward.

The river flows out of Cotswold soon after leaving the blanket-mills of Witney, mills which flourished, according to Dr Plot writing in

Witney, Blanket Hall, now a museum

1677, because 'No place yields blanketing so white as is made in Witney', ascribing this whiteness to the purity of Windrush water. Until the river comes to Witney, apart from a brief meander at the bottom of a few Burford gardens, it has known only small villages fed by springs purified by the porous limestone through which they passed until a layer of clay or fuller's earth meant the water could go down no further and must force an outlet.

The river divides into two channels and comes together again fed by many small tributaries to make an area of marshy ground and water-meadows dotted with tiny islands of willow and scrub, the haunt of mallard and coot and other, more secretive creatures. Their refuge, however, is rapidly being lost to new trading estates, if I interpret rightly the reason for the giant cranes and the unseemly litter of developers I saw there recently, and the wire fences, temporary sheds, rusting oil drums that this kind of enterprise gathers round itself. The little Cotswold villages with their water-meadows, pollarded willows, placid cattle and placid fishermen of the river's higher reaches are another world.

A mile south-east of Witney in the Windrush valley, Cogges, a manor farm, illustrates a continuous settlement for the past thousand years or more until 1974 when a member of the Mawle family sold it to Oxford County Council. It has been turned into a farm museum, not a lifeless collection of bygones but a working farm with animals, domestic fowl and husbandry showing the development from oxen to horses and then to machinery, a collection of waggons and carts including the Cotswold waisted waggon; they have also restocked the garden and orchard with the trees and herbs and flowering plants that once grew there, keeping the house and farm buildings as working units so the visitor can get an idea of the farming of the past hundred years or more.

When I was there in September 1984, there was a threshing machine worked by a steam-engine bright with polished brass and shining paint, the engine chuffing as engines should, the chimney smoking, a pile of coal handy to replenish the firebox. While a number of men fed the thresher with bundles of corn, others collected the grain in sacks, others baled the straw and attended to the winnowing device, a bustling, clanking, smoky process that the young men working the machinery obviously enjoyed, though had they been labourers in the early 1900s they might not have been so cheerful, for these were the years of long hours and poor pay. It brought home to me vividly how many men were needed in the old days for the work on a farm.

Again the river makes two channels, one to the west along 'Emma's Dyke' and one to the east that passes Cogges. A good water-supply was always assured because of the position of the farm at a junction of clay and limestone. The old Langel Common dividing Cogges and

Witney was between the two branches of the river after the original woodland had been cleared, and Cogges grew up on an east-west route which was once the quickest and driest crossing of the marshy alluvial valley bottom, for here the flood plain is about a hundred yards wide. This route has now been lost as a continous track. Church Lane before 1860 went westward between the churchyard and Manor Farm, crossed the Windrush by a ford and connected with the market-place by Crown Lane. John Thorne in his booklet on Cogges suggests this early route may have determined the site of Cogges village.

The pattern of the development of Cogges could serve as an example of how from Saxon times many another Manor Farm developed. Ignoring its prehistory, it undoubtedly had Saxon beginnings, for Saxon pottery has been found in the postholes of a pre-Norman house on the site. The first Norman here was Wadrad, follower of Odo of Bayeux. In the Bayeux tapestry '*Hic est Wadrad*' can be seen. He is in a suit of chain mail, holding a spear and shield, while about him other Normans on foot are carrying off a pig, sacks of grain on a pony and a coil of rope. In Domesday Book we read that Wadrad was Lord of Cogges, though he lasted only about ten years, for another Norman family, the Arsics, followed him and ruled the estate for 150 years. They left a house known as Cogges Castle within a moat, with a priory and a new settlement. A lancet window in the present vicarage is all that remains of the priory. The de Greys followed and built the manor-house on a higher drier site. Evidence of the medieval village can be seen in the remains of earthworks, but by 1423 the village and the ploughland had considerably diminished, perhaps because of shortage of labourers after the Black Death.

Sir Thomas Pope was the next owner, but his family sold it to Francis Blake, a woollen draper who may have been connected with the blanket industry of Witney. There is a memorial in the church showing three marble busts, William and Francis, much periwigged, and Sara, who died in 1707. The family were benefactors to Witney: the Buttercross was their gift to the town, and William Blake left funds in his will to provide a school in High Cogges and Witney.

The Enclosures of 1787 made the greatest changes in Cogges, for from that time onward the farms of the parish were surrounded by enclosed fields, and Lord Harcourt, then the lord of the manor, added considerable acreage to his lands as well as making it more productive. Apart from the recent additions of new housing estates, the landscape then took on the appearance it has today. Each century left its mark on the farm, the roads and the fields, and the Enclosures were the greatest change of all.

The farm was let to the Hollis family who farmed there over a hundred years. They rebuilt, renovated and generally improved the buildings, as is shown by the bills surviving in the Oxford Record Office. In 1877 the Mawle family became tenants and then owners of the estate. Joseph Mawle and his sons were prosperous farmers; one son, an engineer, devised a system whereby water was pumped from the moat to the farmyard, a great labour-saver in those days when every pailful had to be drawn from the well. Finally the last member of the family, the only grandson, sold Cogges to the Oxford County Council in 1974.

With the aid of the guidebook published by the Cogges Agricultural Heritage Museum Association, one can trace the continuity of this homestead for over a thousand years, using the farmhouse, buildings, garden and orchard as a living book and so coming to an understanding of how these farmers lived long ago.

The Windrush once clear of Witney served at least four important mills in the old days, before reaching Newbridge in about five miles and mingling its waters with the Thames.

14 · Painswick Proud

The fifteenth- and sixteenth-century wool-men enriched Cotswold by building and rebuilding churches to the glory of God, using some of the wealth they had acquired through their trading. Northleach, Chipping Campden and Cirencester are amongst the most famous of their towns but there are others of lesser degree throughout the district that owe their Perpendicular towers and lofty naves to the same source.

The wool-men, when they died, liked to be buried in the churches they had helped to build, and to lie beneath monumental brasses. These brasses were made in the Low Countries where the wool-men traded, and they were engraved with effigies of themselves, their wives and families with hands folded in prayer, their merchant's mark as well as information showing who they were and a humble plea to the living to pray for them. The brasses were often ordered during the wool-man's lifetime, the inscription leaving space for the relevant information; this is why in some cases the name has not been filled in.

Nearly two centuries later, when wool was no longer sent to the Low Countries to be made into cloth but was woven in Britain, it was the clothiers who took the wool-men's place as the most important merchants in the nation's economy, but as they mostly belonged to the Age of Reason and not the Age of Piety their gifts to Cotswold and posterity were the houses they built or refurbished so they could live in elegance and style as they became prosperous, and the handsome and often ornate table tombs for their burial which are now such an attraction in the churchyards of the little clothing towns. The clothiers did not seem to be as anxious about their souls as medieval wool-men. 'Merchants', wrote Adam Smith in *The Wealth of Nations* in 1776, 'are commonly ambitious of becoming country gentlemen and when they do are generally the best of improvers', which was very often the case on Cotswold.

Influenced by the new Classical Renaissance which they saw in Bristol and London when they went to the cloth markets, the clothiers smartened their houses with classical façades, sash windows, pilasters, pediments and other elegancies or else built new houses in the fashionable style of the period. These houses – 'town houses in the country' they could be called when they first appeared – are now mellowed by time and much cherishing, and enhance the aspect of any High Street where they have survived, for of all the types of domestic architecture down the ages they most embody good taste, good manners and a cool appraisement of man's need for domestic comfort.

The clothiers also built mills for the processes of cloth-making in the narrow river valleys of the Frome and the Little Avon, and these industrial buildings fitted in agreeably with the landscape because of the local stone used, the good ashlar and those finishing touches of the vernacular which the masons could not resist adding, or which they thought were part of the original concept of the building. Unlike the nineteenth-century mills of other industrial districts, where utility and cheapness were the formula, these south Cotswold mills were no gaunt monstrosities intruding on the landscape but stood up solidly but without stridency, the earlier mills often having the mill-owner's house nearby or even as part of the main building so that dwelling and place of work were practically one. The cottages of the work people often stood around them, though the weavers usually had their cottages on the hillside near a running brook where they could wash the wool and have full benefit of the daylight. The tradition was so strong that mansion, cottage, mill, barn and cow-shed all came under the same rules of good craftsmanship until the recessions of the late nineteenth century; there are hopeful signs of a revival today, for people are becoming aware of the status as well as the pleasure a house of Cotswold stone can bring to its owners.

The clothiers of Painswick also left individual memorials in the form of chest tombs in the churchyard, the quality of the silvery-grey stone memorials enhanced by the yew trees and green lawns in which they are set. The designs of some of these bear a resemblance to the fashionable wooden and silver articles of their daily life, the so-called 'tea-caddy' shape, the 'wine-cooler' and the 'pepperpot', for example, octagonal, cylindrical, concave-sided, some finished with knobs that resemble those on coffee-pots. The tea-caddies are said to be a

Loveday House, Painswick

155

particular Painswick production, the work of the famous stonemason John Bryan, who was responsible for many of the most famous tombs. But whatever their design or ornament, the tops were always heavy enough to deter grave-robbers.

The emergence of the wealthy clothier brought a new kind of customer to the monumental masons of Cotswold: rich, respectable members of a middle and upper class who wanted something more elaborate than a headstone or a classical marble tablet on a wall in the church, something which suggested their opulence and ostentation within the bounds of good taste.

Once there was a demand, there were masons and carvers to meet that demand. They selected a finer-grained freestone for the tombs needing crisply cut mouldings and ornament, particularly for under-cutting, and soon used every possible device in the book that could be interpreted as an emblem of mortality or immortality: the acanthus, shells, skulls, swags, hour-glasses and fat cherubs. The carvers seem to have been endowed with a vitality of exuberance that transmitted itself to the stone, so that the acanthus leaves curled almost voluptu-ously, the swags and tassels seemed to have a life of their own. Ideas poured forth like springs gushing from the hillside, as if a pent-up creative force had at last freed itself. Since the wool-men rebuilt the crumbling Norman churches there had been few opportunities for the stone-carver apart from mouldings, cornices or work controlled by strict rules of design. On the chest tomb a carver could let his imagination run riot, for the stone, by its friable nature when new, tempts the craftsman, and many a young mason must have found it difficult to know where to stop. It is evident from the ornament that some of the masons had served an apprenticeship in the stoneyards of Bristol and Gloucester, where they had access to the latest pattern-books of the period. As the eighteenth century advanced they came to the climax of their skills – and to the end of the period of prosperity for the clothier, as the Industrial Revolution began to cast its shadow over Cotswold.

The tombs are not only a valuable source of information for local historians but examples of fine craftsmanship that in some instances are minor works of art, and this, I think, would have pleased those prosperous clothing families who had lifted Cotswold out of the medieval traditions into the Classical Revival.

The masons doing the work were family concerns, as most busi-nesses were in those days, and monumental masons an offshoot of larger businesses concerned with all forms of building from quarrying and drystone walling to the erecting of churches. However, when it became evident that there was little room left in the churches for new burials, as well as a strong movement for banning them on hygienic grounds, a handsome tomb in the churchyard was the only alternative for those important citizens who were members of the new upper-middle class replacing the old landowning families who had ruled the district for centuries, and this meant that specialists in fine carving began to have their separate yards inside the family concern. One finds variations not only in the shapes of the tombs but in the standard of their decoration between one village and another. Some memorials suggest a rustic craftsman with the disarming innocence about renaissance emblems, others with a more sophisticated attitude that could have come only from one of the big stoneyards of Bristol or London, but all have an individuality of their own, for the Cotswold mason follows his own bent and even when reproducing a pattern gives it an individual twist.

Not many names of these masons have come down to us, but John Bryan was famous in Painswick and beyond for the variety of his designs and the excellence of his carving. He and his brother were also general builders in the Gloucester district, but John was the one who carved the tombs. He was no rustic journeyman, for his work shows a strong Italian influence suggesting he might have travelled abroad in his early years or been apprenticed to a craftsman who had. He had a feeling for lyre-shaped ends to his stone chests, a beautiful form curving outwards towards the bottom, which he embellished and made his own by playing with the design as if it were a melody with variations, but all within the conventions of the shape. His two tombs for the Poole brothers in the Painswick churchyard are as handsome as any on Cotswold or beyond.

Headstones were usually made from a coarser-grained stone as the ornament followed simpler designs. The rough, pitted surface encourages miniature plant life and becomes hoary down the years, with the circular traceries of white and yellow lichen as much a part of the surface as the stone is at one with the churchyard trees, grass and mosses.

These tombs of clothiers and other merchants showed the last flowering or decorative work in Cotswold stone before the traditions of the Middle Ages became outdated. The headstones had less scope for fine work and were used mostly for details about the deceased. The favourite motif was a cherub's head, or group of heads – 'ploughboy faces', John Betjeman called them, with a ring of feathers

round the neck or a pair of inadequate wings. Mostly the faces are podgy, with heavy lower jaws, but it is amazing the difference that can be found in their representation. I have never yet found one that looked as if it belonged to Heaven. It is obvious that the pattern-book design had become blurred, copy being taken from copy until the carving had only a vestigial resemblance to the original design.

Amid all the elaborate tombs to the clothiers in Painswick church-yard is a headstone to Thomas Humlet, who died in 1751, which has a simple outline of his tools inscribed above his epitaph. One of the tools represented, a long-handled scappling axe used for rough dressing, has not changed at all since the thirteenth century, for in Lethaby's *Westminster Abbey and the King's Craftsmen* is an illustration showing a mason holding a scabbling axe similar to the one drawn on the headstone, and the same kind of tool is still used today.

Today the handsome little town of Painswick, so sparklingly fresh in the clear air of the uplands and whose silvery stone reflects the light so on a sunny day that the general impression is of a town bathed in light and air, looks as if it had always been concerned with gracious living. Yet for two hundred years or more it was one of the most important clothing towns in the west. Bigland's *Collections* records, eighty-one headstones and tombs between 1684 and 1829, bearing the word 'clothier' on them in the churchyard, and one must take into account that these were only the employers; their workers must have run into thousands, but workers seldom had any form of memorial to mark their graves in those days.

The earliest of the clothiers of the sixteenth century were in a smaller way of business, this being the age of the undyed broadcloth when the trade was just beginning. It was between 1620 and 1800 that Painswick and the Stroudwater towns became prominent, for it was then discovered that the abounding springs and streams pro-duced the clearest water for dying in the West Country. Stroud was famous for its red cloth used by the Army, and Uley for its blue cloth for the Navy. In an entry in his diary for September 1826, the Reverend Francis Witt noted: 'Machinery and Millworkers bestride the once limpid stream long dyed a deep blue by the processes carried on.'

The Painswick clothiers, the Tocknells, the Pallings, the Littles, Walthens, Pooles, Lovedays and others, formed a community of their

House in Bisley Street, Painswick, thought to have been built by John Bryan, stonemason, for himself

own, intermarrying and sharing social activities and, I expect, with a certain competition amongst the wives as well to display the silks, the expensive teas and the porcelain brought back by the East India Company in the ships that carried the broadcloth from Painswick and the Stroudwater valley on their outward journeys. Painswick's churchyard, with its clipped yews, its tombs which would have been bright with silvery-grey stone newly quarried and carved, and its green lawns, was the town's promenade, a place for elegant sauntering on Sundays, with the ladies displaying fine silks and shawls from the East and the gentleman in attendance discussing the week's gossip and news. The yew trees have attained a magical significance over the years, though this has now been eroded by modern scepticism. Originally there were two dozen planted and more were added to make a hundred, but for some reason or other when counted there never seemed more than ninety-nine, the magic of numbers working its spell to baffle the human brain. To arrive at the correct number one could use one of the modern aids but I doubt if science could kill the legend.

But there is more to see in Painswick than the gracious houses that belonged to the clothiers. It has a series of little streets leading down to the streams where many an ancient cottage now restored and smaller houses of true Cotswold vernacular are sited at varying angles according to the humour of the builder and the space available, for as in many Cotswold villages there is little room to expand on the flat. There is Tibbywell Street and Tibbywell Lane, with a spring now called St Tabitha's Well but which was recorded as Towy's Well in the sixteenth century, when the Painswick people were forbidden to wash swines' entrails in its water. One of the houses in Bisley Street has a Gothic archway of the size to take a loaded packhorse and belongs to the days before the clothiers took over from the wool-men.

Bad times fell upon the clothiers in the early nineteenth century and upon the weavers, spinners, fullers, combers and all connected with the clothing trade. Stroud accepted the new process of steam-power, a more reliable source of power than the old water-wheel, which was erratic in times of drought and flood. The changing fashions were for new kinds of weaves; the old broadcloth was no longer wanted, and new weaves meant new machinery, reorganization of the industry. The clothiers found it difficult to accept the new fashions: they could not believe that their hardwearing broadcloth was no longer bought by the increasing population, who wanted cheaper and more fancy goods. The dyers also had to be more adventurous to meet the new demands. A fancy name given to a colour is no new way of tempting a customer, though modern advertising might like to think so. To quote a few colours from those listed in a dyer's book of that period from a dye-works at King's Stanley: 'Rich French Grey, Light Reddish Mouse, Pompodore Mixed, Rich Corbeau, Plump Crimson, Olive and Eye White'. It would be interesting to see Light Reddish Mouse. I cannot imagine a lady wanting to look like a mouse, and I would like to discover how Plump Crimson differs from other crimsons, but the word Plump may have changed its meaning since those days, as words will.

With the loss of its clothing trade Painswick sank into obscurity in the same way as the wool towns of the north Cotswold, Northleach and Chipping Campden had done after the wool trade came to an end. The population dropped as weavers and other workers moved to new factory centres in the north of England where the Industrial Revolution was on the way; other workers emigrated, some to the United States, and descendants of these immigrants now come back to visit the 'old country' and swell the tourist trade.

Cranham, three miles or so north-east of Painswick, had connections with the clothing trade, and earlier with the wool trade because on the Perpendicular church tower built in the fifteenth century was once carved two pairs of shears, a symbol used by weavers or cloth-shearers at the beginning of the cloth trade in south Cotswold, telling the world that a cloth-shearer or a wool-man had helped to erect the church. This was the device used on a memorial brass to Thomas Fortey, Agnes his wife and Agnes's first husband William Scors, who could have been a tailor or cloth-shearer for he has a pair of shears at his feet. (I think if he had been a wool-man he would have had his merchant's mark as well.) Thomas Fortey, we are told, was 'a counsellor, worthy merchant, upright, true and kindly not inconspicuously known as an unpleasant self-satisfied man' but William Scors has only his shears to show his trade, and of his temper we are told nothing.

In the early nineteenth century Cranham was also known for its crude pottery – flower-pots, pipes, milkpans for dairies and other domestic utensils – and the potters had a reputation of being rough and turbulent men, particularly at election times, when they fought any who were not of their persuasion, or what a local reporter called their 'blue interest'. Probably the local candidates supplied the ale for their supporters, and excessive drink could have been one of the

Cranham Church

reasons for the broken noses and black eyes in stories that have come down to us. They must have been fighting men for this reputation to have been remembered for so many years.

The extensive and beautiful Buckholt Wood which protects Cranham from the north owes part of its name to the Old English for beach, and it was a village famous for its charcoal burners in the twelfth century. The name Cranham, according to the experts, comes from Anglo-Saxon meaning 'the heron-haunting homestead'; the herons must have come from the Frome, a fair flight, otherwise the name does not fit the rather bleak situation of the village on its common with the church at the higher end.

Today and for many centuries past it is not for its clothing trade but for its glorious beechwoods that Cranham has been renowned. Foresters tell us that the finest natural beechwoods on Cotswold are Cranham Woods on the high ground between Cranham and Dursley, concentrated on the inferior oolite, the last western outliers of the natural beechwoods of the downs. This part of east Gloucestershire has the highest rainfall of the county, thus helping to develop a rich layer of humus for encouraging growth. The fine, fibrous roots of the beech drain the soil of moisture, and this, combined with their dense canopy of foliage, keeping light from the ground beneath the trees, causes other vegetation in their vicinity to suffer from drought, particularly in the well-drained soil of the hillsides. This means that the trunks of the trees are not so obstructed by the fret of under-growth, for only a few small plants and thin grasses grow under them, revealing the smooth, sculptured upward flow of the trunks standing out with a silvery-grey lustre to give the woodland form as well as grace.

Closer under the trees one sometimes comes upon miniature delights for the eye, a group of harebells of translucent petals and hair-like stems, or more rarely a cluster of fleshy bird's nest orchids, a saprophyte with pale brown scales and yellowish petals, a strange plant with no green in its stems or buds. One's feet moving along the varying strata of dead leaves may let loose from the deepest layers a rich leaf-mould scent that arouses the cupidity of gardeners who know the value of this natural fertilizer.

15 · Stroud and the Golden Valley

Stroud stands where the four main streams and roads of the Stroud-water clothing valleys meet. It is a place of congested roads noisy with through traffic as well as with its own burden of heavy lorries and other vehicles, and it can be disagreeably windswept, to the pedestrian at least, for the wind seems to blow from north, south, east and west and around corners to assault the unwary and add to the irritation that the noise of heavy traffic, the petrol and oil smells and the general lack of grace can produce in anyone unaccustomed to busy industrial towns. The lower town shows the scars of the demolition of Stroud's industrial nineteenth century. There is the usual crane, looking like the deserted toy of a giant, and the litter of old mill-yards and warehouses, which must sadden any enthusiastic industrial archaeologist looking for evidence of the more recent past, but patience and poking about in these dismal areas, in my experience usually muddy with dirty puddles, broken surfaces and rank weeds, will reveal a few clues to the beginning of Stroud as an industrial area.

The old bridge over the Frome has been reshaped; the once proud front of the Stroudwater Canal Company's offices on the main road has a disused look; the stagnant water of the canal is covered with green scum, while nearby the viaduct and the buildings of a lost railway station have not yet passed to that state of antiquity that erases all poignancy for a lost era. Indeed, Stroud gives the impression of being more interested in the future than in the past and regards the sprawl and litter as part of the development, for it is an optimistic town. And one does get the impression that it is not standing still but is forward-looking and ready to tackle the future, though where it is going it would be difficult to say.

It is allowed
That Stroud
Holds naught that's pretty
Wise or witty

goes the old ill-natured jingle. Stroud may not be pretty but it serves the countryside around as a necessary shopping centre, as one can tell by the traffic being more congested on Saturday when the country people come shopping.

Its site on steep hills with narrow roads, a haphazard lay-out, gives it a character that lifts it out of the commonplace. Whenever it has wanted to put up another building, it has had to consider the terrain, the difficulty of making a road up or down to serve it. I once saw it looking almost beautiful from a train window one autumn afternoon, looking down at the river and the green ribbon of the canal, with every fifty yards or so grey stone mills, while on the northern bank the hillside and its beech trees were lit in a golden glow, a true Golden Valley for those few moments.

In the nineteenth century Stroud, having more initiative than its neighbours Painswick and Minchinhampton, adopted steam-power and so did not suffer catastrophically as they did when the bulk of the cloth-making moved to the north of England, yet this brief respite despoiled the place and robbed it of its comeliness. There was no money or incentive in the struggle to keep alive to build in local stone or to follow the old traditions needing time and money when there were shoddy substitutes to be had more cheaply when they needed additional cottages for workers or buildings for the new cloth-making techniques. Also the get-rich-quick and the muck-means-brass attitudes born of the new idea of progress seemed to point the way to success. The other clothing valleys kept their handsome stone mill buildings unspoilt by grim utilitarian ideas, but these, empty and desolate, were no comfort to the thousands of spinners and weavers, fullers and combers who were left without any means of earning a livelihood, having to fend for themselves as best they could in a world that showed little understanding of their misery. 'The shuttles', as Rudder put it, 'were laid in a silent grave' – shuttles that for three hundred years had worked from early dawn to sunset echoing down the valley of the Frome and its tributaries.

In the old days the army went to war in Stroudwater scarlet; in peace huntsmen wore it chasing the fox, and the Red Maids of Bristol wore it to school, keeping warm in their fine red cloaks; county squires went to church in a coat of Uley Blue, and coarse blue cloth was supplied to the Navy and many a Blue Coat school. It has been estimated that early in the eighteenth century some two to three million fleeces were used in the industry in the Stroudwater valleys alone.

Fortunes were made but many of the clothiers bought land and manor-houses for their own personal aggrandisement and to secure a future in a higher social status for their families. Few attempts appear to have been made to put capital into new inventions that might improve the industry. Not that the workers approved of new inventions that could prune an already over-manned work force and put them out of work . . .

Traditionally the shearers were a rough, turbulent set of heavy-weights who could handle giant clippers that sheared the cloth with twenty-four-inch curving blades. They often worked fourteen hours a day to earn a wage that barely kept them in ale, and they had a reputation for tremendous thirsts and drunken brawling – a natural thirst was intensified by the nature of their work for, when they were working, the air was never free from fine particles of fibrous dust from the shearing. Also to excuse their own shortcomings employers often exaggerated any attempt their workers made to assert themselves, regarding any criticism as revolution. In 1802 a season of great distress may have prompted the writing of the following letter about the new shearing machines sent to Paul Wathen, a man arrogant with wealth and with his position as one of the landed gentry as well as being a clothier: 'Wee Here in Form you get Sheer in mee sheens and if you dont pull them down in a fortnights time Wee will pull them down for you, Damned infernal Dog. And before Almighty God we will pull down all your mills that have Meany Sheer in me Sheens in. We will cut out your Damned Hearts and will make the rest Heat them.' Here is illustrated how the old paternal attitude to employees of the early days of the trade when the mill-owner still lived near his mill and his work people had changed.

Paul Wathen lived at Upper Lypiatt Park, near Bisley, a hamlet which today consists mostly of his house. Originally this was a late fourteenth-century manor-house with outbuildings and a chapel of the same date, but he altered and enlarged it, giving a pseudo-Gothick rendering in 1809, with somewhat sinister undertones. Paul Wathen was a friend of the Prince Regent and soon squandered the family fortunes that his father, a local clothier, had made, for consorting with the Prince and his companions he indulged in all the extravagances of the period. Knowing of this reckless squandering, while they were on the verge of starvation, no wonder the men sent this threatening letter, though it had little effect upon his wild, reckless way of life.

Another wealthy clothier of that time, Philip Shepherd, followed a similar extravagant course but without the viciousness. According

Lypiatt Park's eccentric buildings

to his own confession, he spent £100,000 in three years, in raising and equipping his own troop of Yeomanry in 1795 and keeping a pack of hounds. In the end, he had to flee to the Continent to escape his creditors and being put in jail, while the mills at Uley ceased to work and thousands of workers were thrown upon the parish with no means of support. The era of the Golden Fleece was perishing miserably

'The Golden Valley' is the name given to the Chalford valley, which lies east of Stroud. The Victorian interpretation of the name was because of the gold russet-colour of beechwoods on the hillsides in autumn – hillsides which descend to the narrow valley where road, river, canal and mills are packed tightly together with this cloth-of-gold background, but before that time the term referred to the wealth which was made there when the clothing trade flourished mightily.

In tiers on the hillside, on any available flat space or platform, are the weavers' cottages, the houses, the little churches and chapels, reached by steep, narrow lanes winding up and down in a mizmaze of communication, suitable only for sure-footed mule or pony, lanes which caused the clothier's wives at that time considerable annoyance because no decent-sized carriage with its horses could climb the steep rises. Heavy goods such as stone from the hilltop quarries had to be taken down on sleds, particularly in bad weather, sleds being easier to control than carts or waggons.

Chalford lies four miles south-east of Stroud on the north side of the Frome and covers two square miles. This part of Cotswold is cut into deep gorges opening out westward from the Severn plain, and minor gorges or ravines open from the major ones, while the valleys are deep, narrow and wooded, beech predominating. The parish of Chalford includes Chalford village, the hilltop villages of Brownshill, Bussage, Chalford Hill and France Lynch and the hamlets of Ashmeads, St Mary's and Toadsmoor. Where one ends and the other begins is a problem for the visitor, and, I suspect, for some of the inhabitants. The parish of Bisley lies to the north and is the mother parish of them all, while the parish of Minchinhampton lies south, so within this area was once a great concentration of clothing mills in the valley bottoms shared with the main road, the river, the A419 from Cirencester, the London to Gloucester railway line and the abandoned Thames and Severn Canal, while the cottages of weavers and other workers were perched on the hillsides.

The village of Chalford itself extends about a mile and a half from

Belvedere Mill, Chalford

St Mary's in the west to Ashmeads in the east, and the nearer one gets to Stroud the less characteristic of Cotswold the buildings become. Within the village, or rather spreading out from its centre, is a bewildering collection of ascending stone-walled lanes, and from all of them as one goes higher are breathtaking views of the valley below and the opposite hillsides. Orderliness in the shape of neat rows of cottages, straight roads or straight-edged plantations does not exist in Chalford; its great charm is the bewildering jumble of woods, mills, cottages perched on ledges of rock, some with two storeys in front and one at the back, and the secretive ways about them. Some of the eighteenth-century grey stone mills, with touches of the vernacular to make them seem at home, have been patched and botched with the makeshifts of the last fifty years or more, red brick, crumbling timbers, deserted yards, occasional new workshops flimsy-looking when compared with the old buildings, clean and bright but wearing an almost ephemeral appearance.

The disused canal is fortunately fed by fresh springs so it does not smell stagnant despite the green scum and the overgrown towpath. I heard a fish plop there recently when I ventured through the nettles to look at the water forget-me-nots, the figwort and meadowsweet and the tall ranks of hemp agrimony. It has a strange kind of appeal made up of the irrelevancies of makeshift, decay and new enterprise.

Beyond the post office, men were shoring up a high bank of stone and rubble with wire mesh and drystone walling, a tricky job using the mesh to keep the trickling rubble in place. It made me understand how these steep hillsides in wet weather and after frost could crumble and send an avalanche of loose rock and earth sliding down gathering impetus as it went and covering everything in its path. Living in the Golden Valley must always have had problems of location as well as industry.

There were at least ten mills along the Frome and four along Toadsmoor stream and others lost on other tributaries. Some of these are now used for small industries, but one has become a block of flats, a recognition of the skill of the masons who built it. It stands on a ledge a little above the valley bottom showing a plain but well-proportioned façade, its squarish windows finished with a simple curve at the top looking out over the valley to the wooded hillside beyond. Another old mill, St Mary's, manufactures walking-sticks mostly for the hospital service, one of several mills where this craft is now carried on. Attractions to the industrial archaeologist are a fine iron water-wheel and an old steam-engine whose steam is used for bending the wood.

Stuart's Mill at the foot of Cowcombe Hill was taken by Peter van der Waals, a craftsman who originally worked for Ernest Gimson, who set up a workshop here, keeping alive the Gimson tradition in the making of fine furniture. Today the mill houses a completely modern outfit making bowls, trays and other articles for the gift industry.

One of the most fascinating bits of old Chalford is under the railway embankment, the Black Gutter, visible evidence of the hundred springs of calciferous water which Gloucestershire historians of the past four centuries, according to the Chalford handbook, 'have extolled and which issue from the hillside at this point'. For many years this water was pumped by the local water company to their main reservoir on Minchinhampton Common and returned to Chalford houses, but now in the inexplicable way these utilities are arranged Nailsworth valley gets the Chalford water and Chalford gets Severn water from Tewkesbury.

On a summer morning the best view of the hillside hamlets can be seen from the Cirencester-Stroud road just before it comes into Chalford. Here the small clusters of houses stand out on an open hillside, the sun turning their grey stone into a silvery white so that the buildings look new-made. The siting of these groups has attained a perfection that no planner could have arranged, and one knows that this is the Cotswold that moved poets and artists in the early 1900s and which sometimes seems lost today in an effort to make Cotswold acceptable to tourists. Distance has lent not only enchantment to the view but understanding.

In many ways the Golden Valley is in a state of transition, but there are signs that the potentialities of the district as a residential area and a tourist centre situated in a landscape of unique variety not to be found elsewhere on Cotswold are being recognized. I fancy that in a little while to reside in Chalford will confer a certain status, a Cotswold-plus on the estate agents book. Let us hope it is not tidied up into a trim suburbia.

Bisley no longer deserves the epithet 'Beggarly' of the old jingle which included Strutting Stroud and Painswick Proud. Painswick, with its beautiful houses and churchyard of yews and sculptured tombs, certainly has the right to be proud, but the reasons which may have helped give Bisley its beggarliness have long disappeared and are rarely remembered nowadays, unless some local historian stirs the dust over the memories of the days when the weavers were starving and at war with the authorities over a wage to enable them to subsist. Many hundreds of workless weavers emigrated to America and Canada, and today their descendants come back to look at the place where their family used to live; they fall in love with a regenerated Bisley, its old cottages tastefully modernized and set off to the best advantage with flowering plants and climbing roses.

The churchyard has its own kind of memorial, heavy slabs of stone with greenish copper plates engraved with names and dates so that one wonders how so many clothiers and other wealthy merchants could have belonged to so small a place until one remembers that the church served not only the village but the wide parish covering many miles around. And how were those great slabs of stone, eight inches or more thick and eight feet or more long and three feet wide, brought from the quarry? Each piece would have needed a team of

View of the Severn at Frampton from the Baden-Powell plantation,
Rodborough Common

Double lock-up, Bisley

horses or oxen to move it, and placing them in position must have been a job for a skilled quarryman used to the handling of huge blocks of stone with simple tackle.

There is a reminder of Bisley's poor in the churchyard, a Poor Soul's Light, a thirteenth-century well-head consisting of a circular stone base holding a hexagon with slender shafts and trefoil-headed arches supporting a hexagonal spire with trefoil-headed gable openings, a charming piece of ornamental stonework. It was used to hold candles for Masses for the poor, the candles donated by their richer neighbours to give themselves and the poor who had no one who could afford to pay for Masses for their souls a lift towards Heaven.

Another pleasant little building – as masonry now, for it is no longer used – is a lock-up of two cells with a charming little ogee gable and finial. Bisley parish covers a wide area, so that it does not mean that all the prisoners belonged to Bisley village. Its pleasant exterior would give no pleasure to the prisoners within, for the interior looks cold, damp, dark and as unpleasant a place to spend a night as one could imagine.

Because of its position on the high wolds and because of the site of an ancient track nearby, Bisley parish has a number of Bronze Age tumuli on its hilltop, including one in Golden Coffin Field near Oakridge, the name provoking memories of other prehistoric sites such as Silbury Hill in Wiltshire and Pontesford Hill in Shropshire, where there are legends about golden coffins and knights buried in golden armour, stories that crop up in almost every county in Britain. Money Tump, once a well-known landmark near Bisley, is gradually being eroded. I could not find it at first and asked an old man walking with his dog if he could direct me to it. The reaction when I mentioned the name was amusing. He said he wished he could borrow a bulldozer and search for the money that lay hidden inside it and then he would be rich for the rest of his life. I hesitated to tell him that the legend says it got its name during one of the forays of the Saxons when a wealthy chief fleeing for his life dropped his money as he fled. There is something about the lonely wolds around Bisley that encourages this kind of story. It can still feel very remote from today.

16 · Between the Little Avon and the Frome

Minchinhampton, on a high plateau between the Little Avon and the Frome, had its Market Square made wide enough, in the Middle Ages when the uplands were mostly rolling sheep-walks, to accommodate the large flocks of sheep that were driven through the town. It is a grey, sedate little town, its houses close together as if to shelter from the cold winds of the hilltop. The Market House built in 1698 is supported on stone columns, with the more ancient wooden ones belonging to the time when it was built, in the centre of the structure, and it still keeps its Toll Board of items and prices to amuse visitors. The houses, tightly packed around the Market Square, look deep-rooted and are pleasantly but not excessively Cotswold. They include 'The Crown' with a hipped roof and a first-floor row of nine sash windows, the gabled seventeenth-century front of the Minchinhampton Club House, and Greylands, which has a parapet with vase finials on its eighteenth-century façade. The truncated spire of the church – which I have heard visitors deplore because of its squat appearance and its nineteenth-century decoration of pinnacles – has become a rather lovable oddity now it is mellowed by time.

Minchinhampton, Tetbury, Cirencester, Marshfield and Fairford were mentioned by Defoe in his *Tour through England and Wales* in 1724 as one of the chief cloth towns of south Gloucestershire. Unlike Painswick it never had the gentleman clothiers who later became translated into country gentlemen before the bottom dropped out of the clothing trade but was the home of smaller tradesmen who had difficulty in keeping afloat in the recessions of 1756, 1803 and 1808, when the industry was beginning to move away from Cotswold. Many a man was ruined who set up as a clothier without sufficient

Minchinhampton Market Hall

capital to tide him over bad times. Even in the boom years Minchin-hampton never became as wealthy as Painswick and Chalford, perhaps because there were too many in competition at a time when the demand for local broadcloth was being superseded by more fanciful weaves – 'supertones, seconds, drabs, naps, duffles', as Samuel Rudder described them. In the Gloucestershire Records Office there are documents telling of tragedy, ruin and heartbreak for the clothiers and their families. Some committed suicide, others went to prison for debt. 'We shall have fewer clothiers another year. I hear there was one sent to Gloucester Jail Thursday last,' wrote one clothier at that time, and Minchinhampton had its share of this distress.

It seems to have been the habit of the Victorians on Cotswold to use a church font as a garden ornament when it had been replaced in the church for one of imitation thirteenth-century pattern, and then at the turn of the century for the old fonts to be recovered and re-installed when enlightened churchwardens or clergymen realized that they were of antiquarian interest and part of the original Norman church furnishings, and also that their age automatically made them objects of interest. Minchinhampton's ancient font was found in the rectory garden and restored to the church in 1916.

In 1921 another treasure of the old church was brought back to it, the old Sanctus Bell bearing the inscription 'Dame Alys Hampton 1515'. It was found in Longford Mill but how it got there nobody knew, though speculations at the time were many and local imagin-ation ran riot. It was even suggested that a supernatural force had been employed, but then there is something about church bells, particularly those given as a charity, which conjures up a 'bell, book and candle' kind of magic difficult to define. For country people in the old days their church bells did more than call them to church on Sundays: they were part of the living voice of the village on all important occasions in their lives.

Dame Alys who gave Minchinhampton the Sanctus Bell also gave the townsfolk a common of some 580 acres, 'to belong to them for ever', and it is now looked after by the National Trust. A residential area around it was developed at the turn of the century, a carefully thought out development that was not allowed to get out of hand or encroach on common land. It has a house designed by Ernest Barnsley, and other houses by the Falconers father and son, and they do not take away from the spaciousness of the wide open plateau with its magnificent views and keen breezes but help to enclose it.

The common has Belgic earthworks, a stronghold of the southern Dobunni, and it could be that Caractacus in his forays into Roman-held territory to and from Wales used it as a gathering place or even in the fighting season as a fort. The common is now a playground for the inhabitants of Stroudwater and summer visitors, and it can absorb an astonishing number of picnic parties without appearing overcrowded. It has never been cultivated, and the soil is poor and thin over brash and rock, the sparse grass eroded by too many grazing animals and humans at play. But when dusk falls and the golfers, the lovers, the picnic parties and others have gone home, the common can be one of the loneliest places I know and being left to the sky-enfolded solitudes brings back a primitive fear of emptiness and the demons that lurk in darkness. The passing lights of a car crossing the central meeting-place of roads at Tom Long's Post does little to relieve the silence, and it is not the ghost of Tom Long, the highwayman said to be buried here at the site of many of his hold-ups, but rather an indefinable sense of a more ancient past that comes out of the silence that can hold terror as well as peace.

Less than a mile south, below Ball's Green on the Aven, is Longford's Mill, once owned by the famous Playne family. There is '1705' on a date-stone under a little ornamented window, and another with '1865' below that, the date of a drastic rebuilding and enlarging necessary because of a new period of prosperity when a demand for fine broadcloth flared up again after practically dying out. In 1912 Longford's had another mill built on ferro-concrete piles in the modern style. It is one of the few cloth-making establishments on south Cotswold that managed to survive the competition from the north of England, recovering several times after trade recessions brought disaster to other mills, thus becoming a landmark in the Cotswold cloth-making industry.

Avening lies south-east on the Aven from Longford's Mill, below an area of high Cotswold where long barrows, including Norn's Tump with its port-hole entrance, standing stones called Tinglestone and Long Stone and other relics of the prehistoric past inhabit a lonely area of farm land averaging some six hundred feet above sea-level but feeling much higher. It can be bleak and seldom without a chilly – or an invigorating – wind, according to one's mood or fitness, but it can be a relief to descend into the little Aven valley to the village of Avening and leave the ghosts of past ages to their solitude.

Though the village is in borderland country between Cotswold

and the Severn Vale, it is Cotswold in spirit and appearance with its stone cottages, mill and millpond now disused. The valley has an air of well-being and domestic comfort like most Cotswold villages today but it has had its bad times when the clothing trade declined.

The 1902 restoration of the church was sympathetic, so that its Norman and Early English features are easily picked out. The church also contains a local museum, including a length of Stroudwater Scarlet once made in the local mill and now hanging like a weaver's banner, as worthy of its position in a church as that of any knight who went to the wars, for the weavers fought against tremendous odds of grinding poverty, the indifference of the authorities and the relentless tide of the Industrial Revolution and were defeated. Yet it was their good work which for many years made the country prosperous and renowned for its cloth, and which enriched the clothiers so that many could become part of the landed gentry.

The Driver family of the seventeenth century are represented by some lively Baroque memorials made by Reeve of Gloucester, the sculptor who was responsible for the handsome black marble chimneypiece at Dyrham Park. There is also an effigy of Henry Brydges, pirate and highwayman, who, as the story goes, had to flee so often from arrest that his horses were shod 'hind-before'. If the stories are true, he seems to have been a swashbuckler of the worst type, but with the aid of what used to be called 'ill-gotten gains' he managed to get reprieved and came to Avening to settle down as a respectable citizen, though I suspect his neighbours were not always comfortable in his presence and avoided meeting him at night. Samuel Baldwin of Stroud carved the effigy, a craftsman much in demand at that time who was responsible for many effigies in the early seventeenth century, including the well-known Kingston memorial at Miserden and the alabaster effigies of Herbert Watson and his family in Broadwell church near Stow. I became well acquainted with this memorial because many years ago for a few seasons as I sat in Broadwell church I could see Herbert Weston's memorial and amused myself during dull sermons trying to imagine the life of the family in those far-off times. Samuel Baldwin's sculpture made the Weston family come alive for me.

Tingle Stone long barrow, above Avening

17 · Wotton-under-Edge and the Ozleworth Brooks

Wotton-under-Edge is perched on a marlstone terrace just under the escarpment, as its name implies, in the centre of one of the best view-points in south Cotswold. Today it is an unpretentious little town, and so far the restorers, with their emphasis on the more picturesque and tourist-catching trimmings, have not moved in. The nineteenth and twentieth centuries are more apparent than its eighteenth century past, when it was an important cloth-making and cloth-dyeing town with a great number of mills, dyehouses and all the subsidiary workplaces necessary to the clothing trade. One has to look for the decaying mill buildings by the little streams and tributaries of the Avon, and here one recognizes the extent of its industries from three hundred years ago until the late nineteenth century. E. S. Lindley, the town's historian, gives the number of people engaged in the trade in John Smith's census of 1608 as half the community. Samuel Rudder, in 1770, said there were seven to eight master clothiers, and Bigland in 1831 asserted that there were thirteen clothing mills which employed 770 families compared with sixty in agriculture, but this list does not include small establishments for by then the industry was overstocked with men seeking to make a living in this way. The 1854 Health Report gives only three mills in the parish employing about two hundred hands, showing the dramatic decline in less than twenty years.

The loss of the trade was catastrophic for the town. There were no other industries to take its place, and work on the land was so poorly paid that the farm labourers often had to ask for parish relief to eke out their wages. Heavy work was impossible for the weavers, if there had been any available, for they had been obliged to keep their hands soft, so as to handle the wool, they were not strong, having been brought up to a sedentary occupation, and they were poorly nourished, having suffered a wasting loss of unemployment for years on and off before the final collapse.

In 1825 there were serious riots, the desperate men terrorizing dissenting weavers willing to work for a low wage just to keep their jobs, the masters having the erroneous view that they could increase trade by cutting the wages bill. There was little sympathy or understanding for the weavers workless through no fault of their own, and in January 1826, having determined to teach the rioting weavers a lesson and because they had been lenient with Stroud protesters to no effect, the magistrates inflicted the harsh penalty of two years incarceration in prison, or, as the sentence read, 'in one of the Houses of Correction'.

Wotton was associated from its beginning with the Berkeley family but the town seems to have received few benefits from the association for the Berkeleys were too busy with their private wars, the royal family, Court and family scandals that reverberated throughout the district. They had their own historian who served them faithfully and put the best interpretation he could on their various feuds and fights and misalliances.

In 1384 Lady Berkeley, second wife of Thomas Berkeley the third, endowed the town with a grammar school. Thomas Berkeley the fourth was buried in the church, and his handsome tomb of Purbeck marble and brass shows him wearing a 'mermaid' collar, while his wife, Margaret, has a little dog at her feet with a string of bells round its neck. As well as being one of the earliest memorial brasses in the county, it is one of the finest and adds much to the dignity of the interior of the church.

There was once a large mural of St Christopher over the south door, coming into view as one entered the church, like the St Christopher at Baunton near Cirencester. It was a favourite subject in Cotswold churches, and I wonder if the painters, knowing the hazards of the ancient tracks that must be traversed by traders in Droitwich salt, Mendip lead, Welsh gold and Forest of Dean iron ore, felt that the patron of travellers was the saint best suited to upland churches. The painting was destroyed at the beginning of the nineteenth century by Canon Henry Sewell, who was obviously possessed by the zeal of many clergymen of his time to rid their churches of evidence of their ancient existence and make all bright and new and usually rather commonplace, though at the time the changes were probably regarded as a way of getting rid of outworn superstitious notions of religion.

The painting as shown in Fosbrooke's History depicts St Christopher with all the traditional additions, the great burly figure with strong, bare legs, the giant staff, the Christ Child on his shoulder so heavy yet so small, the fish in the nets, the mermaids, windmill and men on horseback, with a rowing boat and ships on the water. The medieval Church knew the power of good stories to help the congregation cement their faith, to bring religion within the powers of comprehension without destroying its magic, to have saints who comforted as well as devils to fill them with fear. Without being able to read, the congregation could find on the church walls the story of the Christian faith and make it a living thing. Those forbidding boards of later years setting forth the ten commandments of stark 'Thou shall not . . .' never had the same appeal. We are all children when it comes to stories of Heaven and Hell, good and evil, ready to listen and absorb the moral.

Leaving the church and climbing up Church Street, there is a group of almshouses endowed by Hugh Perry, a wealthy mercer and a Sheriff of London who was born in Wotton. He remembered his birthplace in his will, leaving £300 to the town to erect an almshouse with gardens near the church for six poor men and six poor women, with extra money to yield £12 a year to be distributed to the inmates and, a happy afterthought, £1 for an annual dinner for those choosing the inmates. The Perry Hospital, as it is called, is a pleasantly proportioned and picturesque building of six gables facing the street, each gable with its finial and in the centre a charming little wooden-domed cupola. An alley leads through a flat arch into a courtyard where a seventeenth-century chapel stands, a small, venerable building without ornament except for a small, traceried window. Homes for six people and a gallery reached by indoor stairs looking over the courtyard have now been modernized with good drainage, hot water, electric cookers and all the necessary amenities, and without changing its pleasant seventeenth-century exterior. I went through into the courtyard one day in the hot summer of 1984, and there on a bench sheltered under the ancient walls several old ladies and their warden were sunning themselves. I was delighted when they told me how happy and comfortable they were. I think this would have pleased Hugh Perry when he grew old and began to think of a benefaction that would keep his name alive in the place where he was born. And he is certainly remembered today, for the Hugh Perry Hospital is one of the most charming and outstanding buildings in Wotton-under-Edge.

Berkeley House is another interesting building in the vicinity, though not as old as the almshouses, and its name does not mean it

Chapel and courtyard of almshouses, Wotton-under-Edge

was ever inhabited by a member of the Berkeley family. It lost its original Jacobean interior when a speculator bought the building and sold off every possible interesting feature, including a whole room with pinewood panelling painted green and an original set of paper hangings painted in the Chinese style with birds, flowers and trees dating about 1740, which went to the Victoria and Albert Museum in London. There was also a brass and iron firegrate and a chimneypiece surround with applied plaster decorations. An oak-panelled room of earlier date was sold to a museum in the United States. The house has a spiral wooden staircase of the newel-post type. The 1763 survey shows that it was owned by Humphrey Mayo, goldsmith and mayor in 1734 who, E. S. Lindley says, could be the originator of the Chinese Room. The house also had a fine lead cistern considered early seventeenth century, though it could be earlier, and a stone tablet depicting three mother goddesses or *genii loci*, originally found by the roadside near the Chestles area north-west of the parish where there are Roman remains, suggesting that Berkeley House at one time was the residence of someone with diverse interests – one would like to know more of him.

A perambulation around Wotton with David Verey's *Buildings of the Cotswolds* will reveal many interesting buildings, some with eighteenth-century façades and sixteenth-century backs, but the general impression is that the town relates more to the last hundred years or so than the days when it was a busy Cotswold cloth town. Being halfway between Gloucester and Bath, it makes a good centre for exploring Cotswold and the upper levels of the Severn Plain, while all around the town are rolling uplands, hidden valleys and fascinating views of the Severn snaking its way along green meadows, and beyond the river the mountains of Wales.

Two miles south-west of Wotton-under-Edge the hills are cut into two deep valleys, Ozleworth Bottom and Tyley Bottom, both having streams fed by springs issuing from the hillside. Along these streams and their confluence with the Little Avon some fifteen clothing mills once worked, until by 1850 trade had been so reduced that most of them had ceased to function. Looking at Ozleworth Bottom and its stream today, it seems almost impossible to imagine that this narrow valley (with only a rough farm track from Wortley and Alderley for transporting the finished cloth and raw material and a steady pull up a rise to Ozleworth itself) could have held such a number of mills and mill buildings. It is one of the most unlikely sites of an extensive industry I have ever seen on Cotswold. To reach the main road there are several miles of a mizmaze of lanes that only a local inhabitant can unravel, and they, in my experience, find it difficult to direct a stranger seeking Ozleworth church, the Bottoms, the Roman remains and Newington Bagpath and its castle mound all marked so tantalizingly on the map but elusive on the ground.

One of these fifteen mills has the intriguing name of Hell Mill, given to it by John Smith, the Berkeley family historian. It stood where the stream receives the Seven Springs, just outside the old Wortley boundary. It has been suggested that 'Ell Mill' was its proper name, indicating the width of the cloth made there, or 'Hill Mill' because of its situation. It seems possible that rustic wit, which ever likes the play on words, changed 'Hill' to 'Hell', helped by the fact it may have had an unpleasant reputation.

Only a few broken ruins covered with coarse vegetation in the summer, millponds silted up and the arch of a water-outlet remains in Ozleworth Bottom to remind the local historian in search of visible evidence of an industry that once employed thousands of workers. Only the cattle in the sloping fields, a passing kingfisher and other secretive creatures of the wild find refuge here.

One comes to Ozleworth church first through the gates of the lodge of the big house and then via the front of the house itself and into the stableyard, which has a handsome archway leading to the stables and other farm buildings. The little church and churchyard are built inside a circular earthwork like the one at Condicote, probably a 'henge' monument of the Bronze Age, a place of traditional sanctity associated with worship long before the church was built about 1130, as its early Norman features show, a place where a priest came to conduct Mass outdoors on holy days.

The oldest part of the church is a central hexagonal tower in two stages, the upper stage with a two-light window in each face; hexagonal towers are rare on Cotswold. It also has a deeply undercut archway with pierced chevrons across, not along, the order so intricate in its carving that one wonders if the mason held his breath at each delicate point when a fraction of an inch was between him and the spoiling of his work. I have heard it called a crown of thorns because of its many sharp points but this is too fanciful a name, I feel, and was possibly the invention of a Victorian journalist with an aptitude for inventing pretty phrases The interior has the look of a church unloved but cared for as a matter of duty and seems to be sinking back into the past, there being no present or future to keep it living today.

It became a cell of St Peter's Abbey, Gloucester, in 1146, after Roger Berkeley had given the adowson to the Augustinian community of Leonard Stanley, and although there was a restoration in 1875 by the Reverend W. H. Lauder, the medieval additions and alterations of the original Norman church predominates. An American visitor who had asked me to show him some Cotswold churches said to me, as if disappointed, 'But this is not typically English. It belongs to the Continent,' and I had to agree with him, though one could say the same of all our Norman and medieval churches that have not suffered too much from Victorian Restorers.

But there is a 'foreignness' of special charm, a strangeness not only because of its setting in the stableyard of an English country house but because the countryside around it has that same feeling of remoteness from town or highway. I am glad that, though redundant, it is to be allowed to exist as a church, if not an active one, though it did seem a little lost as I wandered within its low church-yard walls which keep several good table tombs within its magic circle. There were cowslips and oxlips amongst the grasses when I last saw it, one sunny afternoon in May, with rooks calling from a nearby rookery and an insistent cuckoo in the distance. In comparison it made the life of the ruined mills along the stream seem of very short span.

But though redundant, Ozleworth's church is in the care of the Historic Churches Commission, whereas Newington Bagpath's gaunt little church stands desolate, stripped of its religious trappings and now for sale (the price quoted £15,000). Amongst the few memorials which have now disappeared was one to a company of poor weavers of the parish. It did not say if they were employed in any of the mills of the district or whether they worked like the early weavers at their looms in their own cottages. Like the weavers, now the church no longer functions it is cast off, though when it was living there could not have been a very large congregation unless there were many more cottages in Newington Bagpath than there are today.

Three miles west of Wotton-under-Edge and on the other side of the Little Avon there is a living antiquity in the Tortworth chestnut tree, which has existed some six or seven hundred years and in 1984 was still putting forth an abundance of fresh leaves. Its appeal is because of its age rather than its beauty, when so many more durable things have perished and been forgotten. It is marked on the one-inch OS map of the district as an ancient monument and has survived wars, floods, famine, bombing raids and the axe of the kind of destroyer who suffers from the itch to cut down an old tree. There may be yew trees that are older, but no other county in England can show a tree known to have been living so many years ago. Travellers of old delighted to write about it, and with each new record another legend has evolved so that it is difficult to disentangle myth from fact.

The fourth edition of Evelyn's *Sylva*, published in 1706, is the source of the story that the tree was living in the reign of King Stephen, but this statement could be challenged for there is no mention of the tree in the first edition of the *Sylva* of 1664. Evelyn also suggested that it could be a boundary tree, but no such record exists

The Tortworth Chestnut

188

as far as it is possible to discover. Chestnut trees are not mentioned in
Dr Grundy's *Study of the Saxon Charters and Field Names of Gloucestershire,*
though ash and oaks are recorded several times as part of a Saxon
boundary. *The Flora of Gloucestershire* of 1944 says the Tortworth
Chestnut is mentioned in Domesday Book. Sir Robert Atkyn in his
History of Gloucestershire (published 1712) speaks of it as an antiquity
in his time: 'There is a remarkable chestnut growing in the garden
belonging to the manor house, which by tradition is said to have
been growing there in the reign of King John. It is 19 yards in
compass and seems to be several trees together; and young ones are
growing up, which may in time be joined to the old body.' Some fifty
years later Peter Collinson, the Quaker botanist, in the *Gentleman's
Magazine,* gave measurements he had taken of the tree: 'Five feet
from the ground it measured 50 feet round . . . the largest part is
living and very fruitful . . . The solid content of this venerable tree
is 1964 feet, but its true geometrical contents are much more.' So
now we know it was a living giant some two hundred years ago.

An article in *The Gardener's Dictionary* of 1807 described how a
garden wall was obstructing the tree's growth and so had been
removed by Lord Ducie and fresh soil applied to the roots, so that
it produced a fine crop of nuts the next season. Throughout the
nineteenth century it engaged the attention of botanists, and then
the interest waned, returning when Elwes and Henry in their *Trees
of Great Britain* wrote that it was still producing nuts. A local *Flora
of Stroud* by Witchell and Stragnall, of 1892, gives its measurements
as forty-nine feet in girth, its branches covering a circle of thirty-two
yards diameter, about one sixth of an acre, a small wood in itself.
When the Royal Forestry Society visited it in 1917, they pronounced
that it consisted of three separate trees, the centre specimen with a
bole forty feet ten inches at four feet above ground, the height being
about twelve feet. The original tree, a large hollowed and shattered
butt, should in their opinion be removed as it was riddled with decay
and a menace to the healthy tree growing up against it.

Today the Tortworth Chestnut shows in a centre a gnarled and
twisted butt with a number of good-sized, healthy trees leaning away
from the main pollarded trunk, so it would seem that Sir Robert
Atkyn's comment that it was several trees together was the true one.
There are records of sweet chestnut trees (*Castanea sativa*) of great
age on the Continent, though no actual date is given, so it would
seem the species has a reputation of longevity and at Tortworth has
found a soil and climate to its liking. The sweet chestnut was one of

the trees introduced into Britain by the Romans, so would it be too fanciful to think that the Tortworth tree grew from one of the nuts or tiny saplings they brought? It must have had some special significance to have been recorded in Domesday Book, as the *Flora of Gloucestershire* affirms, and that would take it back to the eleventh century at least.

18 · Cotswold Ways

One of the best ways to explore Cotswold is to follow the course of its most ancient thoroughfare, the Cotswold Ridgeway or, as it is sometimes called because of its foundation of oolitic limestone, the Jurassic Way. It earns the name ridgeway also because it traverses the high wolds and escarpments between the various river valleys draining into the Thames at Lechlade and Fairford, but both names are modern inventions. The earliest we get to a specified name was in the Middle Ages when the route came into one of the four King's Highways, through routes across England supposed to provide safe passage for travellers: on Cotswold this highway was used mostly by ecclesiastics travelling from one religious house to another or to and from their various manors at sheep-shearing and harvest, wool-merchants buying wool from the local markets and customs men collecting the king's dues from market towns such as Chipping Campden, a town of the Staple, Northleach, Cirencester, Fairford.

The whole of the Jurassic Way covers some two hundred miles from the Humber in the north-east to the Bath Avon in the south-west, and sixty miles of it goes through Cotswold, making many a detour to keep to high ground for easier and safer travelling. Unlike the Roman Foss Way, which was designed and made for military purposes, the Cotswold Ridgeway was a natural way, trodden out in prehistoric times by men and beasts, signposted by ancient burial mounds and with many a later offshoot to meet the demands of new settlements as the centuries passed, Salt Ways to and from Droitwich, Saxon herepaths and droves. Evidence that there was a through way from the earliest days of man's occupation of Cotswold comes from the artefacts found in the burial mounds, the worked flints, polished stone axes, gold ornaments, bronze mirrors and daggers, artefacts made of metal and stone alien to Cotswold soil; we can link stretches of tracks by the bronze hoards and other treasure trove discovered near fords and other crossing places where a ridge came to an end and where, to get onto the next ridge going in the right direction, the traveller had first to descend to the valley; the names of Chapmansford, Chandler's Ford and others tell they were once on a route used by pedlars and itinerants. Today much of the route has become part of the modern road system and can be followed by car, but a leisurely progress is necessary or many a point of interest could be missed, as well as the beauty of the scene. I have known travellers in fast cars drive right through Cotswold and be scarcely aware of it.

The kind of day which shows Cotswold to best advantage is one of sharp contrasts of light and shade, with clouds scudding across a deep blue sky and shafts of sunlight revealing and then obscuring the distant hillsides and middle distances, bringing out a church tower or group of buildings, a silver streak that is a stream half hidden in its poplars and willows, a glow from bronze-tipped barley rippling to the sky, and then losing them again, so that the picture is constantly changing. Strong light brings out the colour of the stone; on a dull day it can withdraw into a muted grey, and then we have another aspect, but still satisfying.

Prehistoric monuments are found all along the route, and a good example of their proximity is where the Jurassic Way comes into Oxfordshire Cotswold close to the Rollright Stones, the only Cotswold circle where the stones make the ring; indeed, recent excavations by the Oxfordshire University Archaeological Society suggest that it has more stones now than it had when the circle was first set up. I have never felt that the Rollright Stones belong to Cotswold in spirit, for no other prehistoric site in the region has this hag-ridden and uneasy aura about it or its way of attracting stories, because local people felt evil influences still haunted the place. Magic flourishes best in dark places, and the essence of Cotswold is its openness; its clear searching light discourages the existence of chimera. Rollright in its legends and atmosphere resembles Mitchell's Fold, a stone circle in Shropshire, which also has its tale of a wicked witch and is also situated on arid soil, being actually on sour, marshy ground. About both sets of stones one never finds the brightly coloured, lime-loving wild flowers growing on the scree that flower around the long barrows. William Stukeley's description of the stone circle written nearly two hundred years ago still applies: it was, he said, of 'stone corroded like worm-eaten wood gnawn by the jaws of time', and a later antiquary called the stones 'leprous' because of their pockmarked appearance. Fragments chipped off were once sold at Faringdon market for £1 apiece as lucky or fertility charms, showing that the local people believed they held special potency. The aspect of the stone circle today is not as dreary as it was years ago when three sides of the enclosure were lined with ragged firs and shabby elder bushes. Maybe it is because at one time Wychwood Forest came up to the enclosure, that some of its reputation for sinister happenings has spilled over.

After passing Rollright, the Jurassic Way went westward to curve round the Evenlode valley on its way to Stow or north of Moreton-in-the-Marsh to regain the Edge at Broadway, following the lip of the hills in a series of roads and lanes to Birdlip by first crossing the head of the Coln valley near Andoversford and then making a swerve to avoid the valley of the Churn. From near Birdlip it had to make a wide detour to keep out of the deep valley of the Frome before returning to the ridge, then to deviate again from the direct line to avoid the valley holding Tetbury; after that the steep-sided coombes between Stroud and Wotton-under-Edge had to be avoided, though of course the actual towns did not exist in prehistoric times. Coming to Chavenage Green the Way, now overlaid by the A46, went past Nan Tow's Tump, a high, round barrow giving rise to the legend that Nan Tow, a local witch, was buried upright, but in the tantalizing manner of legends the reason for this unusual burial is not revealed.

The Way comes into Somerset and the last few miles along the ridge to Lansdowne above Bath. Travellers wanting to reach the sea in prehistoric times would have had to finish their journey by water on the River Avon. It is likely that near here the old trackway met the Great Ridgeway or one of its branches coming from Wiltshire and going on to the lead mines of Mendip or the mouth of the Axe, where there was a harbour for sea-going vessels before the estuary silted up.

A journey along the Jurassic Way today can unfold much more than its prehistory, for, as in other hill regions, Cotswold history was largely determined, until the beginning of the twentieth century, by its land and water lines of communications. The story of the past unfolds as the hills themselves unfold, as one travels along them with an accompanying changing skyline. The Way assisted the passage of invaders down the ages. After the Romans departed and their roads fell into ruin, as made roads will when neglected, the trackways renewed themselves naturally, frost breaking down the ruts made in

Salt Way crossing trackway to Grim's Hill Iron Age fort at Ruel Gate

wet weather and grass growing over them when winter was done. The Saxons used parts as herepaths, and when they became permanent settlers, the old tracks as well as Roman roads served as boundary lines for their homesteads, as Anglo-Saxon charters reveal. The siting of many of Cotswold's little towns owe their origin to the old highway, for charters giving permission to hold a market were issued only to places easy of access to travellers – that is, near an established highway or junction of highways, because of the tolls required by the lords, abbots and bishops who had power to grant the privilege. People using the market to buy or sell needed beds for the night, refreshment, stables for their horses and pack-animals, storage for their goods, so that once established a village with permission to hold a market soon became prosperous, attracting permanent residents as well, and this meant new buildings, perhaps a chantry chapel and other amenities.

As late as the beginning of the coaching era the Jurassic Way and its offshoots were an essential part of the road network, for the heavy mail coaches found the well-drained limestone soil of the hills easier going than the mire and potholes of the valley roads, and from time immemorial until the coming of the combustion engine drovers used them to bring cattle and sheep to town markets, finding free food for their animals and a more leisurely going suited to their trade.

A new through route recently devised and called the Cotswold Way runs from Chipping Campden in the north to the city of Bath in the south-west. This is a modern tourist attraction and a departure in route-making, having been put together for recreation and not grown out of the need of people to travel for essential reasons, and also to ensure that everyone had a right to walk on some part of the hills at least. It is made up of parts of old tracks, modern roads and lanes linked by short stretches of new footpaths or resurrected old ones. It descends into the valleys on occasions to look at this or that point of interest, and it is waymarked to help the walker on his journey. Its users are expected to observe the Country Code, and for the most part, being sensitive to the privilege the new Cotswold Way confers, most of them do so. The Cotswold Way covers some hundred miles, forty more than the ancient Jurassic Way, and is a wonderful modern achievement, brought about after many pains by dedicated people who worked hard to make it possible. It is a route for the walker, and this gives time and opportunity for looking round and lingering at will; also the wayfarers can become acquainted with the shapes of the hills and the changing skyline so that as they travel they can enjoy the exhilarating sense of moving ever onward to journey's end.

But I hope the wayfarer will not resist the occasional temptation to turn aside and explore a lane, a hidden coombe, a steep grassy hillside that does not come into the official itinerary, for the most treasured memories of places can be those we discover for ourselves, to remain for ever a private possession the more precious because we own them only in the mind.

Glossary

ACANTHUS	Plant whose leaf pattern was used as decoration – mostly carved on tomb-chests and capitals.
ASHLAR	Blocks of masonry fashioned with even faces and square edges.
BALK	Ridges of earth between cultivated strips of land.
BANKER	Stone bench used by banker masons.
BANKER MASONS	Men who cut the cornices, mouldings and other stonework of buildings needing special skill.
BEAKHEAD	Norman ornamental design – row of bird or beast heads with beaks often biting into a roll moulding.
BEAM	Handle of breast plough.
BOSS	Knob or stud placed at the intersection of ribs in a vault.
BILLET	Norman ornamental motif – short raised rectangles at regular intervals.
CABLE MOULDING	Norman carving resembling a twisted rope seen on doorways and around the rims of fonts.
CHANTRY CHAPEL	Chapel attached the church, endowed for the saying of Masses for the soul of a founder or guild.
CLAPPER BRIDGE	Bridge made of large slabs of stone, built up to make piers with larger flatter slabs on top as roadway.
CRYPT	Underground room below east end of church.

FINIAL	An ornamental finish to gable.
GARGOYLE	Water spout projecting from wall of tower of a church, usually of grotesque animal or human shape.
HEREPATH	Track used by Saxons as war-path or for travelling. Usually a prehistoric track-way.
HERRINGBONE WORK	Stone or brick laid diagonally instead of flat. Alternate courses in opposite direction making zigzag patterning on face of wall. Attributed to Saxon or Early Norman period.
HOOD-MOULD	Moulding above an arch or lintel to throw off rain water. Also called label.
IRON AGE	Period between 600 BC and the coming of the Romans, AD 43.
LONG AND SHORT WORK	Saxon stones placed with their long sides upright and horizontal alternately.
MISERICORD	Hinged seat of choir stall; when turned up, it provided support during periods of standing during long services.
MULLION	Upright dividing a window into two or more lights.
PERPENDICULAR	English Gothic architecture from about 1335 to 1550.
PILASTER	Shallow pier attached to a wall.
QUOINS	Dressed stones at the angles of a building.
REREDOS	Structure behind an altar.
ROMANESQUE	Architectural style of the eleventh and twelfth centuries.
SPANDREL	The surface between two arches.
SWAG	Carving representing piece of cloth suspended from both ends.
TALLUT	Local interpretation of tallet, a loft over stables or similar building.
TOMB-CHEST	Chest-shaped stone box, a medieval form of funeral monument.
TYMPANUM	The area between the lintel of a doorway and the arch above it.
WAINSCOT	Wooden lining to a wall.

WEEPERS   Small figures placed in niches along the sides of medieval tombs, also called 'Mourners'.

Bibliography

Adlard, E., *Winchcombe Cavalcade*. E. J. Burrow, 1939

Arkell, W. J., *Oxford Stone*. Faber, 1948

Atkyns, Sir Robert, *Ancient and Present State of Gloucestershire*, 1712

Baddeley, W. St C., *A Cotteswold Manor: the History of Painswick*. Kegan Paul, 1907. Alan Sutton, 1981

Barnard, E. A. *Stainton and Snowshill*. CUP, 1927

Brill, Edith, *Life and Traditions on the Cotswolds*. Dent, 1973

Brill, Edith, *Old Cotswold*. David & Charles, 1968

Brill, Edith, *Portrait of the Cotswolds*, Hale, 3rd edition, 1971

Cannan, Joanna, *Oxfordshire*. Hale, The County Books, 1952

Carver, Anne, *The Story of Duntisbourne Abbots*. Albert E. Smith, 1966

Carver, Anne, *The Story of Duntisbourne Rous*. Albert E. Smith, 1968

Clarke, Thomas and John, *Stock Book and Dye Book of Thomas and John Clarke, 1804 21*. Devizes Record Office, vol. VI, 1950

Clifford, Elsie M., *Bagendon; Excavations, 1954–56*. Heffer, 1961

Clifford, Elsie M., *Bagendon: A Belgic Oppidum*. Heffer, 1962

Crosher, G. R., *Along the Cotswold Ways*. Pan, 1976

Dent, E., *Annals of Winchcombe and Sudeley*. Murray, 1877

Derrick, Freda, *Cotswold Stone*. Chapman & Hall, 1948

Drayton, Michael (ed.), *Annalia Dubrensia: Collection of verses in honour of Dover's Hill Games and telling of their history*. 1636

Evans, H. A., *Highways and Byways in Oxfordshire and the Cotswolds*. Macmillan, 1905

Finberg, H. P. R., *Gloucestershire*. Hodder & Stoughton, 1955

Finberg, H. P. R., *Roman and Saxon Withington*. Leicester University College, 1955

Finberg, H. P. R. (ed.), *Gloucestershire Studies*. Leicester University Press, 1957

Finberg, Josceline, *The Cotswolds*. Eyre Methuen, 1977

Gibbs, J. A., *A Cotswold Village*. Murray, 1985. (Reissued as *Cotswold Countryman*, MacGibbon & Kee, 1967.)

Gretton, M. S., *Burford*. 1914

Grundy, G. B., *Saxon Charters and Field Names of Gloucestershire*. Bristol and Gloucestershire Archaeological Society, 1935–6

Hyett, Sir F. A., *Glimpses of the history of Painswick*. J. Bellows, 1928

Jewson, Norman, *By Chance Did I Rove*. Earle & Ludlow, 1952

Knapp, J. L., *Journal of a Naturalist*. 1830

Lindley, E. S., *Wotton under Edge*. Museum Press, 1962. Alan Sutton, 1977

Lipson, E., *The History of the Woollen and Worsted Industries*. Black, 1921

Marshall, Norah, *Blockley Silk Mills*. The Blockley Antiquarian Society, 1979

Marshall, William, *Rural Economy of Gloucestershire*. 1789

Massingham, H. J., *Cotswold Country. A survey of limestone England*. Batsford, 1937

Mills, R. B., *The Strongs and the Kempsters*. Private mss.

Playne, A. T., *History of Minchinhampton and Avening*. John Bellows, 1915. Alan Sutton, 1978

Riddelsdell, H. J., Hedley, G. W., and Price, W. R., (eds), *Flora of Gloucestershire*. Cheltenham, 1948

Rudd, M. A., *Historical Records of Bisley*. John Jennings, 1937. Alan Sutton, 1977

Rudder, Samuel, *A New History of Gloucestershire*. 1779

Rudge, Thomas, *General View of the Agriculture of the County of Gloucestershire*. Board of Agriculture, 1807

Rushen, P. C., *Chipping Campden*. 1911

Seebohm, F., *The English Village Community*. Longmans, 1883

Steane, J. M. (ed.), *Cogges: Official Guide to Cogges based on work done by Cogges Research Committee, 1975–81*

Tann, J., *Gloucestershire Woollen Mills*. David & Charles, 1967

Verey, David, *Cotswold Churches*. Batsford, 1976. Alan Sutton, 1982

Verey, David, *Gloucestershire: The Cotswolds*. Penguin Books, The Buildings of England, 1970

Victoria County History of Gloucestershire, vols 1–3

Warren, C. H., *A Cotswold Year*. Bles, 1936

Waters, B., *Thirteen Rivers to the Thames*. Dent, 1964

Whitfield, C., *History of Chipping Campden*. Shakespeare Head Press, 1958

Wiltshire, Lewis, *Berkeley Vale and Severn Shore*. Hale, 1980

Witts, F. E., *Diary of a Country Parson* (ed. Verey, David). Alan Sutton, 1982

Index

206